REBUILDING FROM BROKENNESS

Don't Let the Breakup Break You

WILLIE JOHNSON

© 2018 Willie Johnson. All rights reserved.

This information contained herein is intended for informational use only. Author/publisher will not assume any liability or be held responsible for any form of injury, personal loss or illness caused by the utilization of this information.

It is always advised to consult your doctor before starting any new workout, diet or training routine. Results will vary from person to person and there is no guarantee for any specific results to be made.

All information presented here is property of Author/publisher.

TABLE OF CONTENTS

Introduction 1

Acknowledgements 3

Chapter 1: Were They Your God 5

   When Did You Give Them The Power? 8

   What Signs Did You Look Past 12

   Always Be an Individual 15

Chapter 2: Loyal or Crazy 21

   Did Your Happiness Matter/Were We Selfish 24

   Fight to Stay Unhappy 27

   Good Excuses for Bad Reasons 31

Chapter 3: Don't Date 35

   Hurt Causes Hurt 42

   You Can't Trust Yourself 46

   Unfair to Them 50

Chapter 4: Complete Disconnect 53

   Deal With You 59

   Take Your Time 61

   Out Of Sight Out Of Mind 64

Chapter 5: Coping With the Pain 68

   You're Not Alone 73

   Write Down Your Thoughts 76

   Handling the Silence 79

Chapter 6: Letting Go 83

Were You the Healer or the Wounded? 89

Taking Responsibility 92

Should We Double Back 95

Chapter 7: Focus On You 100

Stop Thinking about What If's 106

It's Okay to Be Selfish 109

Forgiving Them and Yourself 112

Chapter 8: Finding the Real You 117

Open Your Box/Try New Things 125

Date Yourself 128

Trust Your Instincts 131

Chapter 9: Time to Heal 135

You're Okay 142

Your Strength 145

Start Laughing More 148

Chapter 10: Acceptance 151

What Did You Learn? 159

What to Do Next Time 163

Let Go. Never Forget! 167

About the Author 174

Introduction

Have you ever lost a relationship and felt like your life was over? What about a situation where you caused the breakup, and now feel like you made the worst decision ever? If you've ever been through this, or are currently going through it, let me help you. *Rebuilding from Brokenness* is about dealing with the after effects of breakup. We focus on how to keep a relationship from falling apart, but when it does, what then? This book provides you with the guidance, encouragement, and support you need to rebuild. We all deal with hurt in different ways, but we all go through the same emotions. Not allowing yourself to be bogged down by the negative aspect of a breakup is key. Identifying the cause of your pain, addressing it, and learning from it, is not only important, but relevant. Rebuilding from Brokenness will help you do just that.

If you're going through a breakup remember this, just because you're broken doesn't mean you're worthless. *Rebuilding from Brokenness* is meant to help you see your worth, and why you should find time to cater to your own needs on a regular basis. You may feel like your life is over, but the great thing about rebuilding you is; you can rebuild your life stronger, you gain wisdom, and you learn to love yourself again. *Rebuilding from Brokenness* is a guide to help you get on the right track to do just that.

Acknowledgements

To my mother, thank you for believing in me even when I didn't believe in myself. You have been my backbone, and have been there when I didn't have anyone else. When I told you that I wanted to write this book, you told me, "Do it . . . make sure that you put God first and allow Him to guide your mind and heart to write what He wants you to say." I would like to express my appreciation to Nicola Samuels for always listening to my ideas, and giving me a different perspective throughout the process of completing my dream. All of the conversations about my thoughts, and what I want the book to say, helped push me to finish what I started. Your advice and dedication were a blessing and kept me going when I felt like giving up.

I would like to thank my mentor Dennis Alexander for pushing me throughout the years. I remember when you caught me in the hallway in college when I was supposed to be in your class and you told me, "I thought you were different because it's something special about you young man. You have potential to do great things in this world and touch a lot of people lives." You lit a flame underneath me that eventually turned into a fire. At the time I couldn't see what you saw in me, but I do now. Thank you for telling me that I'm great, and it's up to me to show the world my greatness. To my friend, and brother, Mel Pemberton; you've always helped me bring my vision to life. If I needed your help, you never said no or complained. You were always willing to help. Thank you for helping me bring my vision to life. You are a true friend and brother; I couldn't have done any of my visuals without you.

Sorry A letter to the broken hearted (Written in 2009)

Dear Broken Hearted,

*I'm sorry; words can't describe how much I want to take your pain away. I want to apologize for your hurt and broken heart. Forgive me. I didn't understand what it would do to you until I went through it myself. The late nights when you can't sleep because you're tossing and turning from thinking; after all I've done for them, how they could do this to me. I gave them everything, I gave my soul, body, mind and they do me like this! You scream out **I hate you, I hate you** even though they aren't there. I wanted to spend my life with you and all you did was stab me in the back. I loved you unconditionally and never did you wrong. You try to figure out what you did wrong; you ask yourself, "If I had done this better, would they have loved me more? Would they have cheated on me, broken my heart and thrown my feelings away?" These are the questions that you ask yourself. Then you say, "Oh yeah I'm sorry. I'm sorry I gave your sorry a#% a chance; I shouldn't have ever trusted you, let alone given you my heart; you didn't deserve anything I gave you for the way you treated me." These are the questions and comments you make to yourself. You have to remember, no matter how much pain they've caused you, or how lost you feel without them, if you put God first, I promise you, eventually everything will be alright You have to go through the process of rebuilding yourself. I'm sorry that you had to go through this pain of dealing with a person that wasn't real. The person you fell in love with was a great representative for a bad product. But I understand your broken heart because your heart is my heart; I'm writing this letter to myself. I'm sorry self. I finally understand a broken heart. Let's go on a journey my people!*

Chapter 1
Were They Your God

No matter how much someone loves you, or you love them, there will be problems in your relationship. They will make you angry, maybe even lie or cheat on you. This is a part of life. We are human and we will never be perfect no matter how hard we try. This is why you should keep your relationship with God first. No matter how great things are going, there will come a time when life will come knocking. If you aren't spiritually prepared, your relationship can break you and take you to a place of hurt that will seem impossible to come back from. Understand that you can't put all your trust in a man/woman, because our imperfections will rise to the surface every now and then. It isn't always intentional; it is just human nature. When I think about the title of this chapter, it makes me sad and happy at the same time. I'm sad because I look back over my relationships and I see where I did this very thing. I know it may sound weird that I'm saying this, but most of us have done it, or are doing it at this very moment. Over time, you made them your world without even realizing it. How many of us go to our significant other first, when things go wrong? What about when everything is going right? Whom do you celebrate with first? Whenever anything goes on in our lives, while in a relationship, we tend to go to our significant other first. Every decision we make, big or small, we go to them. If they don't approve of something, it makes you second guess yourself or even give up on it. If they aren't happy with a situation or someone, 9 times out of 10, you take on the same emotions. Don't get me wrong; nothing is wrong with sharing ideas, hopes, dreams, or issues with that important person in your life. As a matter of fact, it is important that you both communicate well and build a deep friendship, because that will be the foundation for a long-lasting relationship. However, when you allow anyone to determine every move you make in life, you are giving them power and control over your life.

It may be a hard pill to swallow but this is where most of our pain comes from when we experience a breakup. We are broken, because we don't know what to do without them. We have allowed them to infiltrate every area of our lives. We have allowed them to come in and take over every thought, every idea, every goal, every dream. Their goals have become our goals, their dreams our dreams. We willingly give up our individuality, so now that they are gone, we feel empty and lost. We no longer know who we are, and what we are about. Don't get me wrong; no matter how you play a situation, if you care about someone, you're going to feel hurt and angry when things don't work out. It's a part of life. However, the hurt and pain intensifies when we give up all that we are to someone else, and then they leave. A few months after I broke up with my girlfriend, I was sitting at home, thinking about what went wrong, and I remembered asking her, "What am I going to do without you?"

She told me, "Live your life." At that moment, I didn't understand the significance of that statement, but it was profound to me years later. I didn't think I could live without her; I felt my life was nothing without her. But, over time, I realized that was the biggest lie I ever told myself. I survived, I moved passed it, and I could live my life; a very happy life, without her. Do you feel like that now, or have you ever felt this way? If you feel like that now, I would like you to know that if I was able to make it through, so can you and you will. When you are feeling this, you have to become grounded in your relationship with God. Focus on putting Him first in your life and everything else comes afterwards. For those of you who are not religious or spiritual, find something that you can focus on, something that will distract you from your present situation, something that will build you up and keep you going. Just find something that works for you.

You can't allow someone to become so influential in your life that their word outweighs yours. This is what happens when you unconsciously make someone your God. There is a line between loving and worshiping. It's your choice if you're going to cross the line of love into the side of no return. Most of us choose to worship someone with our actions because of our love for them. You must change the way you look at your relationships by changing your thought process. Once you change your thought process, your actions will change. Remember this: Your thoughts determine your actions, and your actions determine your happiness.

If you learned how to put someone before you, you can learn how to put yourself first as well. You can do everything to change your actions but until you mentally change, you'll find yourself back in the same place eventually; loving someone so much that they become your idol. Learn to love yourself first, in this day and time you can't afford to give your all and not receive anything in return. People will take advantage of you, and use you up until there's nothing left to give. Once you give everything you have, what will be left for you? Remember love is all action, if you aren't receiving at least a portion of what you are giving, then it's time to evaluate your relationship.

Important Key Notes to Remember:

- You must learn to balance your love for you and them. Know that God is first, your happiness is second and your relationship is third. You have to make sure that God is priority in your life and relationship; if not, then you make room for someone else to be.
- Don't change who you are to give someone what they want. Change can be a good thing, but if it involves putting away your beliefs, goals, or dreams; and if it means that you must be the

compromiser, or the one who sacrifices all the time, then this change is not good for you.
- When you're heartbroken, don't make hasty decisions that are life changing. Take your time to make sure that you have a clear mind and attitude about the situation.
- Understand that a relationship is when two people come together with love, understanding, patience and the ability to compromise. It's not a dictatorship. If you're doing everything to keep them happy and they aren't concerned about your happiness, something is wrong.
- It's better to feel the pain from letting go now, than to give your all just to be left alone, lost and empty.

WHEN DID YOU GIVE THEM THE POWER?

Have you ever been in a relationship where you felt powerless, and no matter what you did or said it was never enough? Was it always about what they wanted and needed? This is a sign that you have given complete control to your partner. No longer are your feelings, wants or needs important in your relationship; it's all about them. The thing is, it never happened overnight; nor was it intentional. In your effort to make the relationship work, you decided that the best thing to do was "compromise." But what we tend to forget is that compromising involves both parties making concessions; not just one. It is not a compromise, when you are the only person that's doing it. After a while, they expect you to be the one to give up everything, and you entertain it. We put ourselves in situations that we aren't supposed to be in, and then get mad when things don't work out the way we think they should. If you continue to do the same thing, you will get the same result. If you continue to allow them to decide the direction of the relationship, then you will continue to be unhappy; you will continue to exist in a relationship that is not good for you. Either way, you must take responsibility for your actions. If you give someone the power, you can't blame, or be mad at them for accepting what you gave to them. Giving someone what they want to keep the peace, or make them happy, is giving away your right to happiness. No one's happiness is more important than yours. You have to pay close attention to the signs; if you don't, they can and will cause havoc in your life.

If you're going through a breakup now, remember, you are stronger than you know. Take this time to focus on you and God. This will help you take back the power you lost when you gave her/him control over your thought process, actions and emotions. I am really good friends with a married couple; unfortunately they went into their marriage with problems. For the sake of their privacy, I will call them Jill and John. They didn't trust each other going into the marriage, and for about three years Jill controlled every aspect of their relationship, and John let her. John felt like he couldn't express himself without having an argument with her. So, to keep the peace, he stopped expressing his concerns to her. If Jill wanted him to do something, he did it even when he didn't want to. He started giving up the things he loved to do and focused on everything that she wanted to do. John stopped chasing his dreams because Jill didn't believe in them. If Jill wasn't happy with it, John wouldn't do it. If she said *no*, then his answer was always no as well, no matter how much something meant to him. He allowed her to become the decision maker in the relationship just to ensure her happiness. This was the turning point in the relationship where she became the head and he became the tail. It wasn't a relationship anymore, she controlled his life, and he knew it, but he didn't know how to change it.

No longer did he feel like he was in a relationship; he felt like he was in a dictatorship. Not long into the marriage, it seemed like everything changed for the worst. Jill was no longer the encouraging supportive woman he once knew. She complained about everything and had little to no interest in anything he wanted to pursue. She would check all of his social media accounts, go through his phone and the phone bill to see who he was calling or texting, and she even went through his email. Jill didn't like him having female friends, even those who had been a part of his life for years, but it was okay for her to have male friends that were there before he came into her life. She would talk to her male friends about everything that went on in their relationship. Well, one of his female friends he confided in knew about the problems he was having in his marriage, and she started to encourage him to pray and stay strong. She would call and check up on him while he was at work, and send inspirational videos and quotes to encourage him to fight for his marriage. It felt good that someone cared enough about him to keep him motivated like that. One day he told his friend that he was starting to have feelings for her, but they both agreed that getting involved would be a bad idea.

One day Jill went through John's email and saw the message he sent his friend. Jill woke him out of his sleep by throwing water on him. She was accusing him of being unfaithful to her. She started punching and scratching him, so he ran into the garage and she followed him. He was trying to hold her hands so she would stop hitting him, but she kept fighting and saying, "Hit me, I want you to." He said, "No" and "I'll never hit you" and "I'm trying to protect myself." She broke away and picked up some weights and threw them at him. He was finally able to get the garage door open and ran to his truck. She came out after him and attempted to beat on the truck window with the weights, but he pulled off before she could. At that moment he realized that he either had to leave or he would have to live in fear and unhappiness for the rest of his life. He decided to leave. It wasn't an easy thing to, do but he decided to put his safety and sanity first, and he hasn't looked back since. Taking back your power isn't always easy, but it is necessary to find your happiness.

Sometimes you have to hit rock bottom before you can see what you are doing to yourself. John hit rock bottom, which was the only way he could take his life back. You can't allow anyone but God, and you, to control your life. As a man, you feel that it would be hard for a woman to control you. You look at it from a physical standpoint; however, control is all mental, and most of the time when the control is happening, we don't even know it. Nobody is meant to be controlled;

we aren't animals. When you're in a relationship, you both give up some amount of control; that's normal. A commitment to each other restricts some freedom but doesn't give you control over one another. When you give them too much power you are giving them complete control over you. Have you ever had this happen to you, or are you going through this now? If you have gone through this, always be cognizant of the actions that got you to that point. If you're going through this now, you have to be willing to fight for you, and your happiness, and take back control over your life, actions, emotions and mind. The only way to do this is if you realize your value. You are worth the time, energy and action of taking back your power.

A Few Ways to Tell If You're Being Controlled

- They don't want you to be around anyone. They seem to want to cut you off from friends and family.
- They make you feel guilty when things don't go their way, for example when you want to chill with your friends or even spend some alone time.
- They tell you that you must earn their trust even when you haven't done anything wrong.
- They are always accusing you of doing wrong, and will criticize you for every little thing.
- They like to make you feel like you aren't enough, like you can't give them what they want, and they talk down to you.
- They make you feel powerless, such as when you go out, you have to lie about who you were with so they won't get upset.
- – They make you feel less of a person when you share good news; it's as if it doesn't matter; they will always find something wrong.

Become the Leader of You Again

- Respect yourself enough to say yes to your needs and wants. You only live your life once; no one can do it for you.
- When you have done all you can to make the relationship work, and it doesn't work out, let it go, no matter how hard it may be. Holding on to something that's broken will only hold you back in life.
- A relationship is meant for two people to work together. If your partner always likes to control everything, you must address that sooner than later. Don't complain about something if you aren't trying to change it.
- Pay close attention to the signs of control.

WHAT SIGNS DID YOU LOOK PAST

It's funny how we look past little things we don't like in order to get a piece of what we want. Signs are meant to guide you in the right direction. They are also meant to keep you from going in the wrong direction. We often will not pay attention to them because our wants outweigh our needs. We are so blinded by the strong urge to fulfill our wants that we choose not to see what will hurt us in the long run. We start to chase the things that we want, and we forget about the things that we need in life. When we decide to start a relationship with someone, the signs that tell us to stay or run are often right in our faces; however, we close our instinctual eyes, and hope they will disappear, but they never do. We often have an idea of what we expect from our partners, but how often do we share those expectations with them? We go around thinking that they should know these things, but most times they don't. Why do we look past things in the first place? This is the real question. Why do we excuse things just to please our wants, knowing that it will destroy our needs? You can't look past something that goes against your core values in life; eventually you must deal with the consequences that will come. Eventually, it will come back and bite you in the butt; the things that you truly need will one day outweigh the things that you want. When you look past signs of caution, don't get mad at the person that damaged your heart; be upset with yourself; you were warned. What makes it easier for most people to look past the possibility of future pain? Some people will look past pain for the pleasure of physical appearance, money, sex, fame or even just to have someone in their life. We look past obvious signs for the sake of searching for love. We are so desperate to find love that we are willing to accept whatever/whoever comes our way. I spoke at an event called, "Removing the Bandages" and one of the guests said her mom told her, "Half of a man is better than no man." I thought about that statement and this very topic came to mind; is this one of the main reasons men and women overlook signs that are obvious? Do some people settle for what is here right now because they fear that what they truly need will never come? Some people are so afraid of being alone that they will look past the lying, cheating, mental, verbal, and physical abuse, just to say they have someone. This type of mindset can destroy a person's life and distort their outlook on love. It's not wise to look past signs that you aren't willing to deal with for a lifetime in exchange for a few moments of pleasure. Waiting for what you deserve, and not settling, saves you a lifetime of pain and heartache. I know that we have to be willing to compromise on some things, but it is insane to blatantly look past things that you know will hurt you. No one is worth you walking into hell looking for a piece of heaven.

Do you feel like you look for love in all the wrong places? If so, then why in the hell are you still visiting them? I'm not talking about physical places; I'm speaking on what you look for in someone that attracts you to them. You can't complain about something that you have the power to change. I understand that we like what we like. But, if the things that you like bring you to a place of pain, and you continue to visit that place, then be mad at yourself. We may look past a sign that tells us they aren't the one for us, but we also look past signs that we aren't the one for them. We can learn to love someone, but we can't learn to fall in love with them. We can't control who we fall in love with, but we can control who we allow in our lives to receive our love. You have to be strategic when it comes to dating. So many people are wolves in sheep's clothing; you have to be able to discern which is which. If you always chase your wants, before your needs, you'll always pick the wolf because you'll never be able to see the sheep.

You and your partner have to be spiritually, mentally and emotionally on the same page so that you can make better relationship choices. If you aren't, you will continue to be blind to the bright signs that are telling you to stay or leave. Life is your teacher and your experiences are the lessons. If you are repeating the same courses it's because you haven't learned the lesson it's trying to teach you. The only way for true growth to occur is by being honest with yourself. Just because it looks good, doesn't mean it's good for you. The next relationship you get into, make sure that you are prepared to work on building happiness together. If they aren't willing to work with you, then you have a choice to make. When someone isn't willing to work with you from the start, that's a major sign of what is to come. No matter what happens from this moment forward, do not look past the signs of future hurt, because you're too busy thinking about present pleasure. That's not how life works; it will never work that way. You must first understand that in order to build happiness, you must first experience it yourself. Together, you will be able to build on the foundation of love that you created.

Key points:

- When you chase your wants and forget about your needs, your life is headed in the wrong direction.
- Focus on you and the things that you need; this will help you see the things that you don't need in your life.
- Never fulfill your wants over your needs.
- Don't expect half of a person to give their all, even if you're giving them all of you. Eventually you'll give up trying to make

them whole. No matter how much you give someone, if they aren't ready for change you're wasting your time.
- It's okay to take your time; rushing into things can open the door to a lifetime of brokenness, anger and devastation.
- People will show you who they are; it's up to you to believe them.

ALWAYS BE AN INDIVIDUAL

A major part of why most people are so devastated after a breakup is because they've lost themselves in the process of building their relationship. They completely forgot about themselves; who they are, the things they like or even what truly makes them happy. When you become so lost in your relationship, and forget about you, it allows you to be vulnerable to losing the very thing that attracted them to you—you. It's so important to always have a sense of self, no matter if you are single or in a relationship. I understand, when you love someone you want to make sure that they are happy; that's a part of showing them love. On the flip side, when you give and give until you have given out; you have to ask yourself, are they willing to give back to you in order to build you up? You spend so much time on making them happy that you forget your happiness is just as important. Being in a relationship with someone doesn't make you whole. We feel we need a relationship to make us complete, but no one can complete you, no matter how sweet, loving and supportive they are. That's why it's always good to be by yourself for a while after a breakup, to find yourself again, and to learn to be happy with you. No one can tell you who you are, how you should be, and what you should do with your life to feel completely happy with you. Never let someone's opinion of you become the reality you live in.

A relationship is a partnership; you build, learn, laugh, fuss, argue, cry and make up. Yes, a relationship is meant for two people to come together and love one another, but it's not meant for them to forget about themselves in the process. It's not a completion of who you are, and what you are. You must be willing to put yourself first sometimes. Putting you first isn't your being selfish; it's you being selfless to self. How can you do for others if you aren't taking care of yourself as well? One way to always be an individual while in a relationship is by spending time with yourself; go out and do things on your own or with your own friends, go places and try new things. Spend a day taking care of yourself and catering to you. As you get older the things you like will change; that's just a part of life, but make it a habit to just do you sometimes. If you're going through a breakup it may be hard, but this is a prime time for you to start this process. You are worth the fight to push through your hurt and start learning exactly who you are again. The pain that you're feeling now will turn out to be your strength later. The longer you focus on you, the easier it will become to deal with the pain of losing someone. You will start to see who you were, who you are and who you want to be. Start doing for you now, and push yourself to do more for you. No matter how hard it may get, remember, you have to do for yourself just as you will have to do for your next partner. Another major part of why we lose ourselves is we take the sense of urgency away from our goals and happiness and put it towards our significant other. We get caught up with supporting our partners, and we put off the things we need to do to support ourselves. It's okay to be a support system, but it's not okay to support someone so much that you put your life on hold for them. If you have children together, then you have to have a different outlook on life. Some things have to be put on hold for the kids, but that doesn't mean you forget about yourself altogether. A successful relationship is a puzzle with many pieces. One of the cornerstones of a successful relationship is supporting one another's goals in life; it has to be a team effort. Most unsuccessful relationships are one sided; one person does all of the supporting and encouraging, while the other does all of the achieving and accomplishing. If you feel like you were the one that took the back burner all the time, your relationship was unbalanced. This may have burned you out and made you feel like you didn't matter. Never allow yourself to be put on the back burner for the sake of your relationship, no matter how much you love them. Your life, your happiness, your goals, and your visions are all worth chasing. Never let anyone, no matter who it is, take your happiness from you. We all want to see our partners happy, but their happiness shouldn't be at the expense of you losing yours. You must put yourself first when you feel you are drowning. Sometimes we have to be our own rescue boat when we are lost in life's sea of ups and downs. If you don't take this to heart and start now, the next relationship you get into will end up being a repeat of your last relationship. You don't want to be left behind because you're trying to push your other half ahead. Either find a common ground in the beginning of your next relationship where you both can find your happiness outside of each other, or you will end up alone and lost once again.

Key points

- Spend time alone to reconnect with yourself. Do things that make you happy. This is the only way to complete your happiness.
- Go out with friends and do things that get you out of your comfort zone.
- Set boundaries at the beginning of your relationship, things you are willing and not willing to do.
- A relationship only works if you both put in the work. You can't build them up if they aren't doing the same. Make sure to receive what you're putting out so that you can replenish what you've given.
- Don't be afraid to say *no* to someone so that you can say *yes* to yourself.
- Learn to put yourself first. Don't hurt yourself in order to help others.
- Love is action. If they are taking, and not giving, then what are they showing you? They are showing you that there wants and needs are more important than your happiness. This means they are the type to be selfish and only think about self.

17

WHAT'S ON YOUR MIND?

Rebuilding from Brokenness

Willie Johnson

Chapter 2

Loyal or Crazy

This chapter will discuss being loyal or being crazy in a relationship. This is not the only way loyalty and craziness can be defined, but it may give you a different perspective. It goes both ways, were you the crazy one and they were loyal to you or vice versa? We have to pay attention to our spouse's actions in the relationship, and we also have to pay attention to ours. You could've been blaming them for something that you were causing, and didn't even know it. Being loyal to your partner is great, but there is a thin line between loyalty and crazy.

Have you ever defined boundaries for your relationships? Things you will and will not do? If not, then how do you know when you've crossed the line from being loyal to crazy? We think it's our actions that define loyalty or craziness, but it's our thoughts. Before every action there's a series of thoughts that lead to your actions. There's a thin line between being loyal and being crazy, and it's first defined with your thoughts and then with your actions. Sometimes we think we're being loyal, when in fact we've crossed over to acting crazy. Hurting yourself on a consistent basis to help your spouse may seem loyal but it isn't. What sane person would continually hurt just to make someone else happy? If you go without all the time, and your spouse isn't reciprocating, it's not loyalty that you're showing, you're being crazy. Giving your all to the relationship, for the satisfaction of making it work for your spouse, isn't loyalty. The only way that these situations would be considered being loyal is when you both are giving and receiving. You both are going without and it's on an even playing field. Yes, someone will receive more at times, but when they give back, that makes the relationship is balanced. We become so comfortable in a bad relationship, we learn to adjust, and exist in our situation. That's not being loyal; that's crazy.

What were your actions in your past relationship? Were you being loyal to your partner, or were you doing things that even your partner wouldn't do? Loyalty may have different meanings for different people, but when it boils down to it, loyalty is commitment, plain and simple. Both partners must be mutually committed to each other, and to the relationship, in order to make it work. Have you ever thought back over your actions and said, "What was I thinking?" Looking back over your relationship, do you think your actions brought happiness, or did they cause more strain on your relationship? We seldom pay attention to our actions and the outcomes they bring into our lives when it comes to our relationships. Forgetting about you for the good of your relationship isn't your being loyal; that's craziness. How do you expect to build a foundation that is sturdy if the bonding ingredient isn't stable? Being loyal is supporting your spouse, not living life on their terms; that's control

A few ways I define loyalty in a relationship

- Having each other's back and wanting each other to do better.
- Telling each other the truth, even when our feelings may get hurt.
- Not allowing anyone else to interfere in the relationship; rarely listening to external opinions or ideas.
- Supporting and encouraging each other's dreams through everything.

A few ways I define crazy in a relationship

- Everything is one sided, they want it their way or no way.
- They don't want you chasing your dreams; they complain about the time you spend on building your dreams. Even when you try to include them in the process, they still not satisfied. They want all of your time, and when they don't get it, it's WW3.
- They don't support anything you do, but want you to support everything they do.
- They don't like when you do certain things; if you do what they don't like, they raise hell but when they do something you don't like and you bring it to their attention, they'll brush you off and expect you not to say anything about what frustrates you.
- Finally, they always want to eat off your plate when they have their own food. If they do this, you should leave immediately. I'm joking, just making sure you're paying attention.

Have you defined your role in your last relationship? Were you being loyal or crazy? Words sound great until it's time to put action behind them. That's when you're able to see if their loyalty has substance, or if they're just blowing hot air. Having a loyal partner is the greatest feeling in the world, because you know that you're not alone. But when you have a crazy partner, you hope and pray for the opportunity to be alone, but you choose not to leave. If you're married it's easier said than done, but God didn't intend for you to get married to lose your inner peace. Marriage should add to your happiness, not take away or separate you from it. Even though you will go through some ups and downs, your peace will still be there at the end. If you're in a marriage, and you're staying true to someone who continually takes, lies, or cheats, you are not being loyal, you have lost your mind. I would never encourage anyone to leave their relationship; that is entirely up to them. What I will encourage you to do is to assess your situation and decide if it is truly good for you.

There are times when the problem is, our loyalty is to ourselves. You can't be in a relationship thinking that it's all about you all the time, and not give your partner the spot light. It's not always about you, and if you think so then that's crazy. How do you expect someone to be loyal to someone who is all about self? If the shoe were on the other foot, would you be okay with it? We must get away from confusing loyalty with craziness. Just because things are hard and you still stick around, trying to make things better, doesn't mean you're loyal. It could simply mean that you don't know how to let go. Holding on to something that isn't good for you can be so devastating to your life that by the time you realize you lost yourself, it seems like life has passed you by, and it's now too late for you. Dealing with pain from someone isn't being loyal. Allowing yourself to go through hurt after hurt after hurt because you made a promise to be faithful isn't being loyal. Overcompensating by loving someone else because you truly don't love yourself, isn't you being loyal. Would you set yourself on fire, jump off a mountain without a parachute, or rob a bank just to prove your loyalty to someone? So why are you breaking your heart, losing sleep, not eating, wanting to give up on life, and thinking you can't live without them? You were good before them and you will be better without them.

DID YOUR HAPPINESS MATTER/WERE WE SELFISH

You did everything you could to make them happy; you put them first, treated them better than you treated yourself, and they still left, lied, cheated, and left you broken and lost. Does this sound familiar? Have you experienced this, or are you experiencing this currently? When you look back over the course of your relationship, does it make you feel like your happiness didn't matter? It seems like they wanted the relationship built around their wants and needs! They didn't put in nearly as much work, but continued to ask for more. They made everything about them, and when it wasn't about them, they found ways to make you feel bad. It's because your happiness didn't matter. You were dealing with a selfish individual. Being in a relationship with someone who's selfish will eventually get to you. No matter what, they will find ways to make it all about them. When you need the spotlight and they give it, they never let you forget it. On the other hand, you can't completely blame them for everything. A selfish person will always show their true colors no matter what. They can't hide it, so it's up to you to recognize it, and address it.

Ways to define a selfish person

- Always wants the spotlight.
- Doesn't like to share but wants you to share everything with them.
- They have many rules but the rules don't apply to them.
- They don't like to see you shine, and will make you feel bad for your success.
- They don't ask about your day, but when you don't ask them, they tell you that you don't care.
- They give you grief every time you want to do something.
- They see every flaw in you, but it's hard for them to see the good within.
- Constantly nags and talks down to you.
- They find it difficult to apologize.

There are different ways you can deal with a selfish partner; you stop giving in to all their requests, you talk to them about it and give them the opportunity to change. The change will not happen overnight, so be patient and give them time but let them know that their actions are causing you hurt and you aren't happy. If that doesn't work, you know what you need to do. It goes back to Chapter 1; you have to start putting yourself first. A selfish partner will always be about self. If it doesn't fit into the guidelines of what they want, your happiness will never matter. The next time you start talking to someone you have to pay attention to the signs, and if you see them, you need to walk away before you go any deeper into the relationship. If not, you'll be fighting for your happiness once again. If you don't make your happiness a priority, don't expect someone else to do it for you.

In some ways, we all are a little selfish when it comes to love. We want what we want and that's all there is to it. Most men focus on the physical, but spend little time getting to know who a woman truly is. By the time, they start figuring her out, they are in too deep. Most women, will go for a man with money but won't pay attention to his priorities, his character, if he's a cheater, liar or if he's even ready for a relationship. We put our love into looks, money, fame, cars, clothes, shoes; basically, anything that can be taken away. When you focus on these superficial things, you're saying that real happiness doesn't matter. When you go searching for, or allow things that can be taken away to bring happiness into our lives, you need to ask yourself, does my happiness really matter? You took what fulfilled your wants, and forgot about your needs, because you were having fun. Now your needs have kicked in and are asking for attention. So when they only give you what you asked for in the beginning, and now you want more (but they can't or won't give it), that's your fault. You can't base your happiness on what someone can take away from you in the blink of an eye. We have to take some of the blame for our own unhappiness in life and stop blaming someone else for everything.

It's okay for you to get the things you want in life, but if you are putting someone before your needs, you're going to end up back in this same predicament; alone, hurt, broken and mad at the world. Yes, your partner can be selfish, but did you ever stop to think that you were being selfish as well? You chase things that aren't permanent, but put permanent feelings as if it can't be taken away. Money, looks, sex and materialistic things create a false foundation for a relationship. When these things disappear, the relationship will crumble every time. When everything's said and done, we have to take our time to check our actions. For every action there's a reaction. What did your actions bring about in your life? Were you being loyal to self, or crazy? Were you appreciated or taken advantage of? Did they put in the work or did you put in the work? A relationship is give and take; if they only give you your wants and you take them, don't get frustrated with them. You have to take the blame for only asking for, or accepting, the things you want. So next time, put your needs before your wants; this stops you from being selfish, and it lets you see if you can truly build a foundation.

Ways you are selfish to "you"

- Only asking for or accepting things to satisfy your wants.
- Putting your love into materialistic things.
- No communicating. (If you don't communicate your feelings, thoughts, needs and wants, don't get mad when they don't get it right when they try.)
- Never tell your spouse you are hurting. (This is the most overlooked action that causes havoc in relationships. We expect them to see what we are hiding and when they don't, we get angry with them.)

FIGHT TO STAY UNHAPPY

Why do we make it seem like we are so happy in the public eye, but when we are behind closed doors, we are miserable? This is the worst form of deceit in a relationship. Have you done this, or are you doing it now? On social media, and in front of your friends and family, you're so happy, smiling and showing everyone a world that you created that isn't real. After all the pictures and videos, there's no communication when you get home. There's no love and affection of any sort, and you're just there with each other. When you fight the truth with a lie, you will always end up with a lie. We will get angry when someone walks out of our lives, but sometimes that ends up being a blessing. When God removes someone from your life, and you go back to them and try to make it work, it's just like you are going to the store to purchase a puzzle knowing that pieces are missing. And yet you still go home and try to put it together. We are so afraid to be alone that we are willing to deal with dysfunction just so we can say that we have someone. Why do we fight to stay unhappy? Why are we so afraid to be alone, or to let go of someone that is hurting us? We have become too comfortable with the mess; we have found our happiness within misery. We justify why we stay by convincing ourselves why we shouldn't leave.

Stop justifying your misery by calling it loyalty. Some of us are so eager to be loyal to our partners that we continually excuse and justify their behaviors. Why put yourself through this type of hurt knowing that nothing good will come from it? We have to stop helping someone find themselves if they aren't looking. We see good in them, and so we try to help them see it, but if they aren't in a place where they can see it, you'll wind up losing yourself in the process. We can't allow our loyalty to be our own undoing. Yes, we are supposed to love, care, guide, understand, compromise and build with our spouse. However, it is important to not lose yourself by forgetting about you; change who you are at the core, or give up your dreams for them to live theirs. Loyalty goes both ways; it's not one sided. Be loyal to those that are loyal to you. The craziest aspect of loyalty to me is when someone betrays you over and over, and yet you still hold on to the good old days. That's a great definition of crazy, holding on to what was good even when it's hurting you. Yes, there were some good times, but if the bad outweighs the good and the bad continues to gain momentum, it's time to let go. That's why we need to learn who we are first, before we try to learn who someone else is. If you don't, you can take on who they are, thinking that's who you are, and when they leave, you hate yourself because the things you do remind you of them. It's because you've taken on their personality and ways of thinking.

**How do you give loyalty without losing yourself?
Here are a few ways.**

- Understand yourself before you get in your next relationship. If you're in one, set guidelines to take time for yourself; it goes both ways. Discuss why you're doing it so there is no miscommunication.
- Stop holding on to the past and live in the present while preparing yourself for the future. Meaning, if you're in a relationship, don't think about what they did, think about what they are doing. If it's on a consistent basis of pain, with no growth or change, you have to decide if your happiness is more important. If you're not in a relationship, learn how to let go of what they did because you can't change it, but never forget why and how they did it. This gives you more insight for your next relationship. You will be able to see the signs more clearly.
- Learn what loyalty means to you and how it would look to you. Loyalty is different for everyone. Find your loyalty boundaries so that you'll know when they have been crossed.

One of the biggest reasons why most of us don't let go of someone that is slowly breaking us down is because we're afraid of change. We don't want to put in the work to really be happy, but we'll put in the work to stay in unhappiness. Because of fear, we'll fight to stay in a relationship that's been dead for months or years, and yet we will complain and complain about it. When something is dead, the only way to bring it back to life is with the help of God, if it's his will. If you don't have Him first, then you will continue to beat a dead horse. I remember complaining about a girlfriend of mine. *She won't do this, she just doesn't get it, I wish she could understand, and so on and so forth.* Until one day God used someone to tell me, "Your situation won't change until the situation within you changes." We always look outside of ourselves saying that's the problem, but yet we never address the problems inside of us. We are the company we keep. We complain and stay with someone that makes us unhappy. The fact is that we're unhappy, and we don't know how to find happiness, or we are afraid to go search for it. This tells you much more about what your true problem is: you. Until you are able to face yourself in the mirror and be truthful with you, your problem will continue.

**The difference between happiness and being comfortable.
My point of view**

- Happiness is when you aren't forced to do things to please your spouse; you want to do them because it brings joy to you as well. It brings you peace.
- Being comfortable is when you have a routine for doing things for your spouse. You don't do it *just because*. You do it because you feel like you have to in order to keep the peace.

No matter how much you lie to yourself to make it seem like everything is okay or was okay, it's still a lie and the only outcome from a lie is a lie. Stop fighting to be unhappy because you're afraid of what is out there. The only way to grow from hurt it by facing it head on. Yes, it will be hard, but you are stronger than you know. Yes, it's good to fight, mentally and emotionally, for someone that's fighting for you as well. When the relationship is over, it's over and we have to accept that. You can fight for something that you both don't want, and choose to stay because you're used to it, even if it causes more harm than good. When the outcome is one-sided, that's when it becomes a problem. You should always fight to find your happiness, no matter how broken you are. When you find the true you, that's when you find true happiness. Happiness isn't in someone else; it's within you and it's up to you to bring it out. When you continue to fight against what is called to be, you're putting your relationship before your happiness. God didn't intend for us to live in unhappiness on a consistent basis, and He will not cause it, but He didn't say that you can't and won't cause unhappiness. When it's over, let it go. You're wasting your time and the energy you could be using to build yourself back up to the man/woman you use to be. Your happiness matters.

Pay Attention to the Signs

- Don't be afraid to let go of a dead relationship. It may be hard, but if you don't let go, it will make your life even harder.
- If they tell you they don't want you through their actions and words, believe them and let it go.
- Don't confuse their wanting you to be happy with their still wanting you. Just because they still do things to help you doesn't mean they still want you. They could be trying to help you get past the pain. If that's hurting you more than it helps, you have to walk away for your own benefit.
- No one can tell you how and when to emotionally and mentally let go; that's up to God and you. The best way to start the process for most people is to distance yourself from them. Out of sight, out of mind.

GOOD EXCUSES FOR BAD REASONS

Have you lied to make your relationship look as if you are happier than you really are? If you have then this section is for you. I've done it before; I knew it wasn't right but I didn't want people to know the hell I was in, so I gave them a reason for why things hadn't progressed. I was more worried about what people would say about me than I was of myself. It took me a while to see it, but my relationship had become nothing but excuses. The sad part was, I blamed myself for everything that went wrong. That's why I always made excuses for my partner's behavior. One of the worst things you can do in a relationship is blame yourself for all of the wrong. Blaming yourself creates a bigger problem. You'll never solve every problem if you always over analyze your actions and take the blame for everything. A relationship is give and take, and not from the aspect of, they dish it out and you take it. It's a team effort; you both have to give and take. When this no longer happens, it means something is broken. You can't make excuses for it and think it's going to eventually work itself out. You have to address the problem and collectively come up with a solution to move forward. If you think back over your relationship, could this have been a major key that caused your relationship to fold?

Most of us don't, or won't do this. We will tiptoe around a problem, and never address it until it's too late. The more excuses you make, the further it takes you away from the solution. The further you're away from happiness, the harder it is to get back to that place. It seems like the majority of society makes excuses because they are afraid of the truth, or because they are worried about how they will look. We forget that everyone has problems. No matter how old, young, rich or, poor! We all have problems. We make excuses for our problems, not knowing that excuses hinder you from finding the solution. Yes, we want to have someone in our life. We are meant to have love in our life. We aren't meant to have hurt, pain, anger and, stress in our lives on a consistent basis. When we make excuses for our problems, we are holding on to what is hurting us. You have to be willing to hurt for a little while by letting go of the person that is hurting you the most. Sometimes the person that is hurting us the most is ourselves. We can cause pain to ourselves by not being willing to change our ways.

We make excuses like

- This is me, and I'm not changing for anyone.
- You have to accept me for who I am.
- I've been this way all my life.
- You either take it or leave it.
- You knew I was this way when we started dating.

These statements are false. If it's not beneficial to your happiness, you can change it. We are just uncomfortable with the changing process, so instead of changing we will make excuses for our behavior. You must let go of all your unhealthy ways; the way you think, talk, argue, etc. Yes, our partner does things that hurt us and make us angry and vice versa. The only way to solve any problem in life and relationship is by admitting there's a problem and being willing to work on it. I don't care how good your excuses sound, they will never be a solution to your problems. Problems will come and go, but the truth will remain. Yes, the truth hurts sometimes, but it's better to attack a problem head on than to waste time making excuses for it.

Why you shouldn't make excuses

- Excuses are lies.
- Excuses prolong the healing process.
- The more excuses you make, the longer it will take to solve the problem.
- Excuses hurt just as much as the problem. When someone makes excuses, and you find out later that it was all a lie, you feel like you wasted precious time and you feel like you can't trust them to tell the truth.
- Behind every excuse is a hidden truth.

I have a friend—for the sake of privacy, let's call him Joe. Joe was in a relationship with the woman of his dreams. Everything was going good. She cared about him and, he cared about her. Every now and then he would get angry over the smallest things. Joe was controlling and he did his best to hide it until he knew the woman was all in. Well, life started to take a turn and it forced the revelation of who he truly was. Every time his anger would show its ugly head, he would try to turn it around on his partner. He never physically harmed her, but mentally and emotionally he would, and that's just as bad. He never owned up to his problems; he just made excuses for them. One day Joe was told, if you don't change your ways, your ways will change your life. He was told he would lose the woman that he said he loved so much. He never took the advice. One day she came home and said it was over.

His actions and excuses caused him to lose the very thing he always dreamed of. He never dealt with things, and he always made excuses for them. An excuse without solutions hurts a relationship more than it helps. No more excuses; they create more problems and over time will make you lose sight of the true issue.

Key points

- Focus on the solution to your unhappiness, not the cause. Learn how to build yourself up when you've been broken down.
- Your happiness should always be a priority in your life. If you don't take care of yourself, no one else can. To be healed, you have to be willing to start the process of healing.
- Stop making excuses for why you haven't changed, and start making decisions regarding what you need to do to change.
- Your life is based on what you think and do. You can say all day that you want something, but in order to get it you must first take action.
- Face your fears and stop making excuses. You only have one life to live. If you make excuses for every reason not to do something, your life will pass you by.
- Time waits for no one; it doesn't care about your excuses, your hurt, pain or brokenness. Time will continue to roll on without you. If you don't want to be left behind, stop making excuses and start making plans to get you out of the hurt you're dwelling in.

WHAT'S ON YOUR MIND?

Willie Johnson

Rebuilding from Brokenness

Chapter 3
Don't Date

A friend of mine was married for over ten years. He divorced his wife after he caught her cheating. He didn't give himself time to heal, or the time to get rid of that emotional baggage, or time to move past what happened. Instead, he jumped into a new relationship nine months later. After only six months he called things off. He started dating another woman a few months later, and called it off after a year. This went on for about five years until one day I told him, "The problem you are having is not the women you get with. It's you!" He looked quite surprised because, in his mind, he was convinced *they* were the problem. He was holding on to the pain from his broken marriage. He never got over how his wife hurt him, so he took this emotional baggage into his other relationships. He had trust issues. Until he let them go, he'd always find something wrong with everyone else! All the complaints he had with each woman he dated were the same. He never trusted them.

Taking your time to start dating gives you the ability to open up again. Most importantly, the timing has to be right. I told him the only common denominator in each of these relationships was him. At that moment he was able to see that he wasn't over the hurt of his failed marriage, and he had to make a change. You can't disguise pain, or get rid of it by displacing the source of your pain. That is what you attempt to do when you get involved with someone else without taking the time to heal. Not only did he hinder his healing process. He also added more pain to his situation. Until you identify what your issues are, and take all the time you need to address them, you will always find yourself having these recurring problems in every relationship. Alone time isn't always bad if you're using it correctly. If you're truly searching for the answers, you won't have time to dwell on the pain. You will be concentrating on rebuilding you. If you take time to build a better you, you will find that you are strong enough to do it! Focus and stick to working on you.

Dating too early can potentially break you even more and devastate the individual you're dating. We have to look at the entire picture when it comes to dating too early. It's mostly not for us. It's for the individual we are bringing into our dysfunctional world. They deserve to know how jacked up you are! They should have the opportunity to decide if they want to deal with it! That's only fair, even if they decide to give it a try. You need to know that you're not ready for a relationship, and tell the truth about it. Build a friendship first without any physical or emotional attachments. When we are broken ourselves, we can misread the signs that the universe is showing us. We can take a person that maybe is meant only for support to be our next relationship. If the next person that comes into your life is meant to be your future spouse, you can destroy your chances by moving too fast and not first dealing with the mess. *This is why you have to take your time and not date* so that you can be clear on the signs that are being shown to you.

Bringing someone into your life too early can set you back emotionally and mentally. Just because you feel lonely doesn't mean you should bring someone into your life. You can have someone with you at all times and still feel lonely. This feeling of loneliness does not come from your being alone. It comes from the emptiness you are feeling from the breakup. Remember, feeling lonely doesn't equate to being alone. Dating too soon is more harmful than helpful. We tend to be more selfish and not understanding. We feel like the victim, so we are always in defense mode! We have to protect ourselves from further damage. When we don't like something, even if it's good for us, we may dismiss it. Often we look into things more than we need to, which causes more problems. We may miss out on things that can be meant for our good because we are blinded by our own pain. Mentally, we are so messed up. We truly don't know what's best for us, and we don't really know who we are at this point in our lives. You can become your biggest supporter or worst enemy. When you're broken, most of the time you are your worst enemy. In the next chapter, I will discuss how time can break you, if you don't deal with pain correctly.

Not dating until you're truly ready helps you and your potential partner avoid unnecessary pain. When you date and you're not ready, those mistakes, unresolved issues, and emotions from the past will continue to rear their ugly little heads. It takes time to get over everything that you have gone through. This is why you have to take the idea of spending time with yourself so seriously. Not dating until you're ready isn't punishing yourself. It's saying; "I know that I'm not ready, and I will not allow anyone else to deal with my emotional baggage." You have to change your present, so you can enjoy your future. The more time you take in addressing your current issues, the easier it will be for you to get back into dating. Not dating doesn't mean you cannot go out there and have a good time. It means you shouldn't put yourself into a position where you get emotionally involved with anyone. If you start dating too soon, you may realize one day that the relationship was not what you wanted. You may realize that this person may have been a rebound, and it may be hard to get yourself out of that situation. You have to understand that healing takes time. No matter how strong you think you are, when you're broken, you're broken. You have to free yourself of all that baggage before you decide to walk into someone else's life. It's okay to have friends. If you open yourself to something that you are not ready for, you're asking for trouble that you might not be able to handle.

Key Points

- Do not date until your heart and your mind are on the same page.
- When you date and you're not ready, those mistakes, unresolved issues, and emotions from the past, will continue to rear their ugly little heads.
- Don't force yourself into something you're not ready for; it interrupts the healing process.
- Be smart with your time; use it wisely. Focus on a better you; this will help you fix the broken you.
- You can't disguise or get rid of pain by displacing the source, and without dealing with it first. You will have to face it head on either now or later. It's up to you!
- The past is the past. You can't change it, but it can help you change your future. Learn from the mistakes; see the path the relationship took you down, and never walk that way again.
- Understand that it's going to take time. Be patient with yourself; it's going to be okay.
- Remember, you can learn something good from every bad situation. Identify what you could've done differently. If that situation comes up again, you will know how to handle it
- It takes time to get over everything that you have gone through. This is why you have to take the idea of spending time with yourself so seriously. If you don't use your time wisely you'll find yourself years from now dealing with the same issues. If your fears are making you unhappy, don't be afraid of facing them.

HURT CAUSES HURT

You can't help someone when you aren't able to help yourself, but you can hurt someone when you're hurting. It's unfair for you to bring someone into your life when your hurt is consuming you. Often, they end up paying for the hurt that was caused by someone else. This is what I call "*The Cycle Of Hurt*". Your hurt causes someone else to hurt, and the cycle will continue until you break it. It's okay to have friends that support you on your journey of healing. You will need them to get through this. But, you have to set personal boundaries and ensure that you do not cross them. This will take lots of effort on your part, because this is a time when your level of vulnerability is at its highest. Situations that you were able to handle before may be a bit more difficult to deal with at this point. Those that you spend time with have to be aware of your personal boundaries, and they must be respected. This does not only protect you. It protects them as well!

You may not be aware that you are causing them pain, because you are unaware that you're still hurting. You are blind to others emotional state because, you are so caught up in yours. You don't intentionally hurt them, but pain is consuming our mind and heart. It's hard to give anything more than what you're feeling and thinking about. Hurt causes you to be so afraid of adding more pain to your life. You unintentionally hurt others just to protect yourself from feeling the pain. Your foundation of love is too unstable to try and build a relationship on. Not only is it prolonging your process of healing, but it's completely unfair to the other person. This is a time where you have to be selfish and not give any part of yourself away. You're not whole mentally, or emotionally, so it's best that you are by yourself so that you can mend your brokenness. When you are broken and you try to love, you will only be able to give what you have, which is pain, anger, and brokenness. No one can help you get past, or over, anything until you decide that you want to change. People can give you advice or make suggestions, but no one can make you take action to change your life.

I had a friend that went through a tough time trying to deal with his breakup. He had a good friend that was always there for him. You could tell that she was in love with him. Slowly they started spending more time together, and things started moving really fast. Friendship quickly turned into a relationship, and he started talking about marriage. We all told him that he needed to slow down because he wasn't ready for such a big step, and that he was going to hurt her in the long run. He ignored our concerns; however, later on the reality of his situation dawned on him. He began to question if this was what he wanted. He started treating her differently without realizing it. In return, she started to pull back and eventually they broke up. He was really hurt because he lost her support, but the situation devastated her. The experience affected her so badly that it changed her. She became suicidal and almost took her life. She was able to bounce back after some time.

Although, he welcomed the love and support that she brought to his life, he was not emotionally ready to take on the responsibility of a serious relationship. He was so caught up in the positivity and happiness that she brought him that he unknowingly disregarded her feelings and the effect of her losing him would have on her. If you are not careful, you will prolong your hurt while causing someone else pain. There are times when you may think you are with the right person, but the timing may be wrong. Even with the right person, a relationship can end badly if you have not addressed your emotional baggage. Healing has to take place before you can safely move on. If you truly care about someone, you will not put them in a position to be hurt. Even though you have to focus on yourself at this point, it doesn't mean you should hurt others in the process. This is another example of why you should not date during the healing process.

The biggest mistake most people make when they are hurt is getting physically involved with someone else. It's so true when they say sex clouds your judgement. You can confuse good sex with love, and it happens all the time. Soul ties are real, and if you don't understand them I suggest you do some deep research on what soul ties are. Soul ties are spiritual connections that are made during sexual intercourse, in close relationships and when we vow to do something. Have you ever been going through a breakup, and it seems like you're starting to heal and feel better about where your life is heading? Then you make the mistake of having sex with your ex and you end up exactly where you began? It's because you've reconnected with them, and it brought back those old feelings. It's because every time you have sex with someone, you leave a part of you with them and they leave a part of them with you. This is why you have to make sure to control your desires. They can truly hurt you more than they will help you.

Key Points

- Your hurt is contagious, and if you bring someone into your life while you're still infected with it, they are bound to take on the hurt. You have to be emotionally quarantined so that you can take care of the infection of pain. Don't be selfish and bring someone into your mess; you wouldn't want them to do that to you.
- It's unfair for you to bring someone into your life when your hurt is consuming you. Often, they end up paying for the hurt that was caused by someone else. This is what I call "The Cycle Of Hurt." You can only give what you have; that's a heart full of hurt and pain.
- To stop the cycle of hurt in your life, you must be up front with whoever you're spending time with about your mental and emotional state. Let them know that you aren't ready for anything more than friendship and stick to it.
- When you're not whole mentally or emotionally, it's best that you are by yourself so that you can mend your brokenness. Your having someone in your life is a temporary patch for your hurt. You'll eventually see that you can't fill the void in your life with anyone other than God.
- No one can help you get past, or over, anything until you decide that you want to change. People can give you advice, or make suggestions, but no one can make you take action to change your life. You can have all the advice in the world on how to heal. It will start to happen when you use the knowledge that's been given to you and act on it.
- If you are not careful, you will prolong your hurt while causing someone else pain. Healing has to take place before you can

safely move on into your future. When you bring pain into someone else's life, you have to remember, what you put out into the universe will come back to you. Always be cognizant about your actions, even in your hurting stage!

- Soul ties are real and cannot be played with. Soul ties are spiritual connections that are made during sexual intercourse, in close relationships, and when we vow to do something. The only vow you need to make is when you're getting married. Watch who you connect with. One night of pleasure can equal a lifetime of pain

YOU CAN'T TRUST YOURSELF

When you are healing from a broken heart, you can't trust yourself to do the right thing or make the right decisions. This is a vulnerable time, and what you may be feeling at that moment may change. Have you ever noticed that when you're hurt, you will do things you wouldn't normally do when you're in your right state of mind? I have definitely experienced that. I can look back and say, "I must have been crazy to do some of the things I did when I was going through my process." My decisions were based on pure emotion. I didn't see how wrong I was until my blinders were taken off. I felt like the world was against me, and I was against the world. I was fighting a battle and my opponent was myself. Every good move I made was countered by a bad decision. I thought I knew what I wanted when I really didn't. I couldn't trust myself to do the right thing. Emotionally, I thought I was doing okay, but I was lying to myself for so long that I started to believe it.

I convinced myself that I was ready to move on, and that I could handle a new relationship. I wanted to experience love again. I wanted to have someone around me again, someone that I could call whenever I needed to talk, someone that I could rely on, who could also rely on me. I wanted to feel needed again. In my mind, I knew that it was too soon. In my heart, I wanted to have that again. After multiple failed attempts, I realized that I wasn't ready for a relationship, because I wasn't emotionally prepared to deal with one. What I wanted at that time was something to fill the emptiness inside. I missed having a relationship, and I hated being alone. I had gotten used to having someone in my life, so it was hard to not have that anymore. I realized that what I was feeling was loneliness, but I was never alone. It took a while to appreciate that it was okay and normal to feel lonely sometimes. It is a natural part of the healing process. This is when having a good support system comes in handy.

I started focusing on the important people in my life. I started spending more time with them, and that took away the loneliness. I had to learn the difference between feeling lonely and being alone. I always had my close circle of friends to lean on. If I didn't feel like being at home, I would call them and go spend time with them. I used these relationships as a means of getting over the loneliness instead of facing it head on. In order to address the loneliness I was feeling, I had to understand that this was a natural feeling that accompanied a breakup. I had to accept it, and know that this feeling would diminish over time. I continued pouring myself into activities that uplifted me as an individual and helped me focus on what was more important which was getting myself emotionally and mentally prepared so that I could move on when the time was right.

You will learn with time that being alone isn't always bad. Sometimes it will make you reevaluate yourself and your actions. Being alone will teach you about you, so that you can start to trust yourself again. When you are by yourself, you are forced to deal with life and not push it to the side. Even though you may be hurting, you still have to live. You can't give up on life because you feel like you lost a part of it. I understand the feeling but you have to be honest with yourself; that is the only way you can survive this. Giving up will get you nowhere, so don't just sit around thinking about the pain. You have to find a way to face it. You can try your hardest to cover up you hurt, but it will not go away. Pain is something that you have to work on. Find the purpose of why you are here. You were surviving before they came into your life, and you'll survive without them. That's the bottom line with no sugar coating! You are hurt, but you can bounce back if you work at it!

You need to allow yourself time to slowly get back to focusing on yourself. You have to let time be your best friend at this moment by using it wisely. What intensifies hurt, pain, and anger? The more you think about something, the bigger it becomes in your life. If you don't like what you are thinking about, then you need to change what you focus on. You have to face your hurt head on. There is no way around it. The main thing you have to do is put God first in your life. When we are dealing with emotional and mental hurt, we have a source that is more powerful than counseling, medicine, alcohol, and drugs. That source is God. I don't care how much you try or think you can control emotional and mental hurt. Pain is stronger than you are when fighting alone. If God can help me through it, he surely can help you through it. All you have to do is be willing to put in the hard work. You can get past your hurt and use it to make you stronger.

Key Points

- When you are healing from a broken heart, you can't trust yourself to do the right thing or make the right decisions, because you do not always think clearly. The way that your mind is functioning when you are hurt isn't going to be the way you think when you've healed from your brokenness. Your emotions are all over the place. One minute you want to be in a relationship and the next you want to take time out. It's just best that you be by yourself. Deal with you, before you put your hurt off on someone else.
- Emotionally you're jacked up. You will think that you're okay, when you're not. We all lie to ourselves just to make it through the day, but eventually you'll start believing your lies. When you are broken, you have to be honest with yourself. That's the only way you will move forward with your growth.

- You have to pay close attention to your emotions. They can have you feeling like you are ready for something that you are not, especially if you aren't used to being alone or if you are very uncomfortable with being alone. Would you walk over a bridge that's broken? No. You wouldn't! So you shouldn't allow someone to walk into your life when you are broken. It's just as dangerous as that broken bridge.
- Your main focus needs to be on mending your life, not bringing someone into it. Loneliness is a hard pill to swallow, but it's necessary for your healing to take place!
- Loneliness will teach you about you, so that you can start trusting yourself again. When you are by yourself, you are forced to deal with life and not push it to the side. Loneliness doesn't mean that you are alone, and you have to remember that. *Most of us hate dealing with pain so we try to do things, or have someone around all the time to take our minds off of it. You have to understand that it will not go away until you deal with it. It's best you handle it today so that you can live a better tomorrow.*
- Pain is something that you have to work on by finding the answer to why you are here. You have to find out why you went through this. Why do you feel this way? Why didn't you listen to your inner voice or why am I afraid to face myself? You have to be willing to do what needs to be done today so that you can build your tomorrow. Happiness is earned, not given! You have to work at happiness. The only way to do that is by working on how to fix the pain in your life. All of this will help you get back to that place where you can trust your thoughts and your heart.
- You need to allow yourself time to slowly get back to focusing on yourself. You have to let time be your best friend at this moment by using it wisely. Make sure you are reading things to build your mind. The mind is fighting for your healing process. If your mind is weak, your actions will be weak, and your emotions will follow. You have to strengthen your mind so that you can start to trust your actions again.

UNFAIR TO THEM

Trying to move on before the time is right, will also have a negative impact on the people you get involved with. If you are not in a position to emotionally be there for someone else, then it would be selfish to introduce them to the emotional mayhem that was once your life. It is selfish, because you are only thinking about yourself, and what you want at this point. Even though you know that moving on may be too soon, you do it anyway. When you realize that you have made a mistake, getting involved with this person, it will be too late. They are already emotionally involved and invested in the relationship. They will be hurt in the long run. Now you have created a situation that will have a negative impact on someone else's life. Unfortunately, some of us have to leave a trail of broken hearts before we realize that what we are doing is dangerous to those we come in contact with.

You may be wondering how you can avoid getting involved with someone else while you are going through your process. After all, you will meet people that you are attracted to, and you will fall for them. The answer is simple really. It all goes back to spending time with yourself and your support system. Stay away from situations that allow you to meet new people. If you are trying to avoid getting involved with anyone for a while, why would you put yourself in a situation that allows you to do that? This is like an alcoholic who decides to go to a bar by himself for happy hour. Not a very smart idea, is it? This is no different. You should not put yourself in a position that you know would not be good for you or the person that you meet. You have to get to that point where your thoughts are not just about your own well-being, but the well-being of others as well.

The hurt and pain that you felt when your relationship fell apart, may still be fresh in your mind. Always keep that in mind when you decide to invite someone else into your life. Think about how you felt and how disappointed you were. Then think about how you are hurting them and how you will make them feel. You have experienced or may still be experiencing these emotions, so why would you impose that feeling on someone else? I remember very well what that pain felt like. I also remember that I have put others through it, because I never considered their feelings. Everybody experiences hurt at least once. It doesn't mean that you have to be the one to put them through it. It is not easy to avoid meeting people. It is even harder to stop yourself from falling for someone. You have to be aware; know where you are in your healing process, and keep the feelings of others in mind.

How would you like it if you started dating someone and realized they weren't over their past? I know I wouldn't. It would feel like they took away my choice of sticking around or walking away. Let's say you go to the store to purchase something and when you get to the counter, you realize that it is damaged and yet the cashier says, "Oh no, you must have broken it when you picked it up." How would that make you feel? Like you couldn't trust the store, right? That's exactly how someone would feel if you didn't tell them about your mental and emotional state. Could you blame them? You get them all excited about something new, but you're still dealing with old issues. You have to be cognizant of your actions when someone else is involved. The way things affect you is not the way it affects others. Sometimes you have to be unfair to yourself to be fair to someone else. Life isn't always fair to you, but that doesn't mean you have to treat others the same. Treat others how you want them to treat you.

Key Points

- Your actions can build someone up or tear them down. If you aren't going to add value to their life, you need to walk out of their life. It's that simple.
- Just because you are lonely, it doesn't mean that it's okay to use someone to help you get past your loneliness. That's unfair to them and you wouldn't like it if they did the same to you.
- If you are not in a position to emotionally be there for someone else, then it would be selfish of you to introduce them to the

emotional mayhem that was once your life. Karma is real and whatever you put out will come back to you.
- If you are trying to avoid getting involved with anyone else for a while, why would you put yourself in a situation that allows you to do that? It's very simple. Stay away from your weaknesses.
- Everybody experiences hurt at least once; it doesn't mean that you have to be the one to put someone through it. Don't cause someone to feel what you are feeling, if you don't like it.
- You have to be cognizant of your actions when someone else is involved. The way things affect you doesn't mean it will affect them the same. You can devastate someone to the point that you make them give up on life. Would you be okay with something like that? I hope not!

WHAT'S ON YOUR MIND?

Willie Johnson

Rebuilding from Brokenness

Chapter 4

Complete Disconnect

Why is complete disconnect so important when starting the process of healing? If you're halfway in and halfway out, you'll never give yourself room to grow past your current emotional state and attachment. When you decide to move on, trying to "remain friends" isn't healthy for either of you. Breaking the physical and emotional connection between both parties is necessary in order for the healing to begin when you decide to let someone go. You can't continue to communicate with them, spend time with them, or check up on them. You have to stop all aspects of communication. The biggest mistake most individuals make is trying to be friends after the break up. At this point your emotions are still involved which leaves you open and vulnerable to even more pain and confusion. I remember a time when I was dating this young lady, and she decided to call it quits. She wanted to move on, but she wanted us to remain friends. I had to be honest with myself, because I knew I wouldn't be able to handle knowing that she was seeing other men. The pain from completely disconnecting was hard. I wanted to call her all the time, but I knew that in order for me to let go and move on, I had to remove myself from the situation.

You called it quits for a reason. Whatever it was, it wasn't working. If you decide to let go of a relationship that wasn't working, there is no need to stick around for a friendship. Not now anyway. That may or may not change in the future. For now, you need to stay away. Many times we hold on to a relationship, because we have grown accustomed to our situation. We don't want to deal with the hassle of starting over. When you get fired from a job, do you go back and ask to volunteer your time because you don't want to let go of the good times? Sometimes you have to treat a broken relationship like you would a job. You figure out what you did wrong, what you could have done better, and prepare yourself to move on.

If you decide to remain friends after a breakup, you need to ask yourself if holding on is helping or hurting you. I held on to something that was breaking me into a million pieces by the minute, but I stuck around while trying to put myself back together one piece at a time every day. My pain was outweighing my pleasure, so my happiness was unbalanced. Are you allowing your happiness to be unbalanced because you are trying to work within the perimeters of your broken relationship? Are you staying in something that makes you feel like you're in a box with no windows or doors? Do you feel stuck and don't know which way to turn? Well, I suggest that this is the time to step back and figure out what the problem is.

There are times when you may need to take a break, a period of time when you temporarily step away, time to assess your relationship, your needs, and decide whether those needs are being met. A break isn't always bad; sometimes a break will allow you to see what you truly have and that you shouldn't let it go. But on the flip side, a break may help you to see that this relationship is no longer working for you, and that you need to let it go and move on.

This can become more complicated when kids are involved, but it can be done. If you and your partner can't get along, then you have to distance yourself from them so that you can get rid of the anger and/or frustration that comes from the hurt. You have to be willing to move past the pain, and this will take time. A good start is to limit communication to child-related topics. Physical encounters should be for dropping off and picking up the child. Remember when you have children, disconnecting isn't just for you, it's also for them. It's not fair for them to have to deal with your pain. Don't allow your ex to use your child to get you to see them or do things for them. You run the risk of falling back in the same old routine that got you to this point. Don't allow them to interfere with your growth in any way. You have to protect your emotional state, by any means necessary, no matter what others may think of you.

Disconnect with someone if required

- Cut all communication; unfriend or block social media connections, and delete pictures and text messages from your phone.
- If you find out that your ex is still hanging out where you used to go together, find new places to go. This isn't to make their life better; this is to make your growth easier.
- Don't talk about what was good to others because this will keep the wound open after the breakup.
- Whenever you find yourself thinking about them a lot, distract yourself by doing something uplifting and/or fun. Be your own motivator.

DEAL WITH YOU

Dealing with the decisions you made to get you to this point can sometimes be unbearable. When you're sitting at home thinking about all the sacrifices you made for your relationship, but to have it fail anyway, is a hard pill to swallow. However, this isn't the time for you to beat yourself up. This is the time to figure out what you did wrong, so you can correct the mistakes and move forward. You can't allow your decision or someone else's decision to walk away, control the way you live your life. You have to understand that a breakup is for you to get away from the situation that is causing you pain. We can get so caught up in the person we love, that we forget how to focus on us. We are so used to doing everything to make them happy that we forget about our own happiness. Living life to please someone and forgetting about yourself isn't the way God intended relationships to be. When you do this, it stops you from growing and gaining the happiness you deserve. It's so hard for us to get past losing someone, because we have intertwined our happiness with the happiness we bring to the life of another. No matter if it brings us unhappiness, you have to understand that your happiness is just as important as theirs. When you give up your happiness, you lose your self-worth. Your hurt often comes from you not knowing what you're going to do without them. This is the perfect time for you to evaluate what's important to you. Most of the time you won't know because your happiness has depended upon pleasing them. You can't allow pain to hinder you from growing. If you stop and think about what you have given up, and what you have received in return, you will see that the relationship was unbalanced.

When dealing with yourself, you have to first learn what brought you here emotionally. I learned over the years that we will find ways to cope with pain, as long as we're familiar with it. That means if you're with someone and they continue to do the same thing over and over, you learn how to ignore the pain and put it in the back of your mind. This can be fatal to your emotional state. We allow people to do a lot of things that hurt us all in the name of love, so when you get to this point in life, dealing with you and your choices, it can make you feel like it's all your fault. Even though you may not be totally at fault, you have to take full responsibility for your actions and learn from your mistakes. Never let someone make you feel as though you were the sole cause for the pain that you are going through. This is only true when you allow them to continually hurt you. You should always grow from negative experiences. You have to be willing to break the thought pattern; change the way you go about things; focus on what makes you happy, and stop allowing others to control the way you feel. We all have choices to make; if we don't make them, someone else will make them for us.

Even though you're going through a hard time emotionally and mentally, that doesn't mean you have a pass on life. You have to make sure your focus is on point. You're at that point in life where you can build yourself up or continue to tear yourself down. You either will learn from it or continue to make the same mistakes and decisions. Your next step is up to you; are you going to move backward or forward? When it comes to making a change in life, you have to take things head on and face your fears. I lived life on the edge until I was pushed off and I was left to fall by myself. It was up to me if I hit rock bottom or I spread my wings and fly. I chose to fly. So what is your decision? I know I'm asking you to do something that may seem impossible because of where you are emotionally and mentally, but you can't use that crutch forever! Eventually you're going to have to make a decision, up or down. The only way to build anything in life is to lay a strong foundation and build upon that. What is your foundation and will it be strong enough to support the life that you want to live?

Five Things you can do to release the old you while building a new you.

1. Make God the priority in your life.
2. Devote 15-30 minutes a day to planning your goals and how to achieve them. Visualize your greatness.
3. Step outside your box. Start doing things that makes you uncomfortable in order to push you into becoming a better you.
4. Allow for some "me" time, at least twice a month. Learn to use your time wisely. Only do things that are improving your life, emotional state and the way you think.
5. Laugh a little. They say laughter is good for the soul. If you experience happiness within, the rest of your life will follow suit!

TAKE YOUR TIME

Time heals all wounds only if you allow time to do its job. I've run into so many people that will get out of one relationship and jump into the next one, without giving themselves time to breathe and get back to where they need to be. You have to take time for yourself to refresh your thought process and figure out who you are post breakup. This is especially important when you are letting go of a relationship that you've been in for many years. You need to spend time by yourself, loving yourself, and being completely happy with your own company. This is very important when putting your life back in order. Take time to figure out the things that are important to you. Get back to searching for what you want for yourself. Finish the things that you started to work on that you never completed. Most importantly, start working on your dreams again! You need your space so you can fly and explore your world again, because we often lose ourselves in others and in our relationships.

Most people think that a failed relationship is a waste of time, but I see it differently. A failed relationship is only a waste of time if you don't learn from the mistakes you made while in it. Never look at time as being wasted if you gain something for the time spent within the situation. Spending time with yourself can be the best medicine when you're lost and don't know what direction to go. I've found that meditating on what you see yourself doing and writing down a plan improves the way you feel about yourself, your outlook on life, and your overall self-confidence. Remember, you survived before this relationship, and you will survive, even though it's over! Yes, it's easier said than done, but you have the power to do it.

When you're taking time for you, you have to learn how to put yourself first. You have to make your happiness and peace of mind a priority. You have to make a decision to give yourself some "me" time everyday no matter what. You set this time aside to build yourself up to a place where you are comfortable with the way you see yourself and feel about yourself. After a breakup, you are your first priority, so you need to evaluate everyone and everything that is utilizing your time, but not giving anything in return. How can you be good for someone when you're not even right for yourself? This is why time is so important when you are heartbroken. Figure out how you would like to spend your time with you. This gives you the opportunity to get to know yourself emotionally and intimately. It doesn't matter how long it takes, because there is no time limit on self-growth.

If you look back over your past, if you're a people pleaser, you'll see how you've taken time away from you and gave to others without thinking. Then, when you needed help or wanted someone to do something for you, you couldn't find anyone. Most importantly, in your relationships, if you are a giver, you often find yourself with someone who is a taker, and vice versa. The best way to make things better for you in your next relationship is by having a balance of giving and receiving. Yes, it's okay to give of yourself as long as you have others giving to you. This allows you to have a balanced life and not feel like you don't have enough time for yourself because you're always doing for others. This is the time for you to take time out for yourself and make your life more important to you. Learn who you are, why you are here, and start doing it. When you get in your next relationship, make sure that you both are taking time for yourselves and focusing on what you want and need.

You have to learn to say *no*; it's for your own good. Be organized and plan ahead. It helps you to effectively utilize your time, and if you stick to it, it forces you to take time out of your busy day to spend with yourself. If you do this regularly, it will become a habit and you won't have to think about it anymore; you'll just do it. Taking time for you is so powerful in so many ways. When you do this, it will show you how important your needs are and why you should practice fulfilling them on a regular basis. You make time for others, so make time for yourself. Stop burning yourself out by being the "yes" person and start saying "no." A no for someone means a yes for you. Time waits for no one, so you can't waste it.

Key Points

- Time heals all wounds only if you allow time to do its job. You have to take time for self if you want to truly grow in the right

direction. The longer it takes for you to focus on self the longer it will take for you to heal.
- You need to spend time by yourself, loving yourself, and being completely happy with your own company. So many people are so afraid to be alone that they will never give themselves time to breath. They've lost themselves over the years and they may be afraid of the journey they will have to take to get back to the real self. It will be hard work, but it has to be done if you want to truly be happy.
- Never look at time as being wasted if you gain something for the time spent. As long as you are learning while you're alone, you're using time wisely. If you stop learning, that's when you're wasting time.
- You have to make your happiness and peace of mind a priority. This will seem very hard to do at first. If you're used to putting someone else's happiness first, you'll feel lost, but don't give up on finding your happiness. It takes time, but if you leave your mind open to trying new things, you'll eventually find what you're looking for—you.

The best way to make things better for you in your next relationship is by balancing giving and receiving. Don't give so much that you don't have anything left for yourself. If the other person gets mad that you need time for yourself, you need to reevaluate your relationship. You'll be stepping back into what you were working to get over.

OUT OF SIGHT OUT OF MIND

I never knew how important this statement would be to me in my time of heartache. When my ex left me. I wanted to be in her life so bad! It didn't matter if it was to be the fallback guy or whatever she needed. Fortunately, she forced me to let go because of the way she treated me. At first I was mad, hurt and confused. But later on, I realized that she did me a favor by pushing me away. If I had stuck around, it would have prolonged my hurt and hindered my healing process. When a person is out of sight, it is easier for you to get them out of your mind. Most of the time you'll be doing good until they call or send you a text message. This is why disconnecting completely is so important. If they have no way of communicating with you, you will not think about them as much. You will think of them less over time. If there are no children, that makes it much easier. This isn't you being mean! This is you protecting your heart and giving yourself time to heal!

If you Google "out of sight, out of mind" it is defined as: You soon forget people or things that are no longer visible or present. You can't let them go if they are still around and you are still communicating with them. You need to put as much distance as possible between you and them mentally, emotionally and physically. Most would think that the only way for the idea to work is if you don't see them. Nope! You are so wrong for a few different reasons. Have you ever thought about someone and they called? What about when you're talking about them to someone else and they call? It is power in your thoughts and your tongue. You have to get them out of your head and stop speaking about them for it to work. They can be out of sight, but the power lies within your thoughts. The out of mind portion is the most important aspect of this equation. This is what you need to focus on first, getting your mind stronger!

Whatever you think about, you speak it! Whatever you speak, you want to do it! These things go hand in hand. If you don't guard your mind, it will take you back to the place of unhappiness because, you were comfortable in it. Your mind will have you present, when your body is absent. If you don't occupy your time with doing productive things, you'll find yourself making excuses for why you need to talk to them or see them. You have to make sure they are out of sight and truly out of mind. Your happiness depends on it. You have to give yourself time to breathe and grow. Now, don't get confused. They can be out of sight and out of mind, but if you aren't using your distance from them productively, you'll find yourself years later still thinking about the maybes! It's best that you are making progress while you are in your alone state. Build by yourself and you'll learn how to live by yourself.

The main reason why you need to make sure they are out of sight and out of mind is to give yourself the opportunity to find yourself again. It opens up room in your life for you to grow for yourself. You have to use this time to find you again. Also to find the things that matter to you the most and how to get past your current mindset. Out of sight, out of mind is your way of taking your power back and not having to fight for it. So yes, make sure you don't have any way of communicating with them. Don't go to the same places. Stay off social media! Also tell your friends not to talk about them if they see or hear anything about them. Your mind needs this break to build it back up, to be strong for you again. You only have one life to live. You shouldn't waste it on thinking about someone that is no longer in your life. You live, you learn, and you move on. It's easier said than done, but it is necessary for you to become whole again.

Key points

- You have to take care of your mind when it comes to your breakup. If you don't, it will take you places that you don't want to go. That's why it's best to distance yourself from them.
- You have to stay away from your source of pain. No matter how much you miss them. If they do not want to try and work it out, you have to keep them out of your life.
- The mind is so powerful; you have to take control of it. All of your actions stem from your thoughts. If you keep them in your life while they are talking to someone else, your mind can and will make you want to do things you wouldn't do in your right state of mind. You have to walk away for your peace of mind.
- You have to make sure they are out of sight and truly out of mind. Your happiness depends on it. You have to give yourself time to breathe and grow. When you are holding on to someone

and they don't want you, it's as if you are feeding your mind with more hurt and refusing the cure.
- You have the power to change your life by changing your mindset. Being with someone isn't more important than your feeling whole again. It's okay to let go and love yourself again. That's the only way to move forward! Let go, learn, heal and live again.

WHAT'S ON YOUR MIND?

Rebuilding from Brokenness

Willie Johnson

Chapter 5
Coping With the Pain

Coping with pain can be really tricky. Out of pain comes growth, wisdom, and understanding. Pain can also bring out the worst in you resulting in a change in your actions, the way you treat others, and the way you approach life. Pain can make you or break you. You have to find the most positive way to deal with your pain. Alcohol or drugs won't do it! Getting into another relationship won't do it! Having sex with as many people as you can won't do it! These are all temporary fixes. After these things come to an end, the pain will still be there. When you mask the pain without dealing with it head on, you can make your life harder and the healing process longer. Breakups are painful, but ask yourself this: What hurts more? Staying, or walking away? Think about the reasons you left and how you would benefit if you stayed. Putting those reasons at the forefront of your mind, will help you cope with the pain you're feeling. You have to decide that no matter how long it takes, you are going to get past this. It's easier said than done, but each of us has strengths beyond our wildest dreams. We don't give ourselves the opportunity to tap into it.

When you're in pain, you'll do almost anything to take it away. If you listen to your pain, you will find yourself on a downward spiral. It will feel like the pain will never end. You must stay on top of things, when it comes to dealing with the hurt and pain post breakup. You may feel that no matter what you do, you can't get over this! Believe me, this too shall pass! I was in a really bad emotional and mental state after my last breakup. I felt devastated, and as if my world was ending. I couldn't sleep, and I couldn't eat. I thought about my failed relationship constantly. I stopped doing everything that made me happy. The pain was so unbearable that I didn't even want to leave my apartment. I would lie in bed and cry myself to sleep. I would wake up crying as if I couldn't let it go until one day, I was sitting in the dark. I was thinking about what went wrong. I realized that it wasn't that I *couldn't* let go. I didn't want to! I was holding on to the very thing that was causing me so much devastation. The pain of my breakup!

Are you holding on to your pain? I want you to stop reading for a second, and answer these three questions as honestly as you can:

1. What is hurting you the most?
2. Have you forgiven him/her and yourself?
3. Would you take him/her back if he/she asked you to?

By answering these questions truthfully, you are giving yourself a bird's eye view into where the pain comes from. It's always best to deal with your emotions as they come. Don't allow pain, anger, and frustration to build up! That's a recipe for disaster! Deal with the hurt head on. Ask yourself the tough questions. Talk to people that aren't biased and get a different view on life. You have to be willing to do the hard things today, so that it becomes easier for you tomorrow! If you don't deal with your pain, your pain will deal with you. I remember talking to a young lady that was newly divorced. Her ex-husband broke her heart, so she decided to treat every man the way her ex treated her. She did not allow herself to heal, nor did she know how to channel her pain. Her solution was to inflict pain on every man she encountered.

She became blind to the pain and destruction that she was causing. She couldn't see that the road she was heading down was the very road that she was trying to avoid. The energy you put out into the universe will come back to you. On one particular day, she was having an okay day. Emotionally she was feeling a little bit better, but she still had a lot to deal with. As she was out doing some shopping, she saw a man staring at her. He looked familiar, but she didn't know who he was. Finally, the man walked up to her and said, "I'm sorry for everything that happened between us." At first she didn't recognize him. It was her ex! He'd lost weight and changed his life around. She broke down crying. He grabbed and held her until she stopped crying. At that moment, she let go of all the hurt, anger, and pain she dealt with over the years.

Pain can destroy your life, or it can transform you into a person of strength and courage! It's all about how you deal with pain. You can't allow it to take control of your life because eventually it will ruin your life. No matter how hard it may be, remember, you can and you will get past it. Like I said before: "You can go to counseling all you want, and you can take all the drugs and alcohol that you can bare, or you can have sex with everyone that you meet. At the end of the day, pain will still be your best friend if you don't move past your pain." You have to decide that no matter what happens, you are going to take steps toward a better you. You do this by focusing on your strengths and not your weaknesses! Your thoughts create your reality. If all you're thinking about is pain, hurt, and your weakness, that's all you're going to bring into your life. Change your thoughts, and you can change your life.

YOU'RE NOT ALONE

You are not alone! Even when you're physically alone, and there is no one to talk to, you're not alone. When you're feeling overwhelmed or when you think your world is crumbling around you, you have to go to the only one that will be there when you need Him. God! This is the ideal time for you to find your relationship with God. It's times like these when you learn who your true friends are. One thing that makes life much easier is when you stop fighting against yourself. You have to decide that you're not going to beat yourself up. When you're alone, take the time to re-evaluate your life and your relationship with God.

You have to spend time building or rebuilding your relationship with God. If you don't believe in God, then focus on what or who you believe in.

Most people will go from relationship to relationship, because of the fear of being alone. You have to learn to be alone physically, so you can reconnect with your higher power spiritually. That is our number one problem! We will not give God enough time to do what he needs to do to get us to where we need to be. People will always let you down, but God won't! A great question to ask yourself is: Why do I hate being alone? You need to figure out the "why" and when it started. It's always good to get to the root of a problem, so you can figure out a way to fix it! I didn't like being alone because I didn't want to deal with the pain in my life. I hated feeling that void when someone left. I felt incomplete and empty without having someone around. I continued hopping in and out of relationships until I was forced to step back and rethink my life. There was a period of time where no matter what I did, I couldn't find anyone to fill this black hole in my life. My biggest fear became a reality! I was sitting in the dark and alone in my living room. I knew I had to make a change. I knew it had to start at that very moment if I wanted to change my mindset, if I wanted to get over this fear of being alone.

I've heard broken people talk about being alone while someone is lying right next to them! How does that happen? How can you be physically in someone's presence and still feel alone? It's because no one can fill a spiritual void in your life. No matter how good they treat you, or how much money they have when you're in this dark place, you have to go to your only source of light: God. I completely understand your feeling and I will speak from experience. You'll never feel whole until you turn to God to fill that place of emptiness! Stop allowing others to come into your life thinking you can use them to take the loneliness away. They will never do for you what you want them to do. They will never fill the void in your life. That feeling of emptiness that seems as though it won't go away. I was able to get to my place of Zen, by disconnecting from the world. I got off social media, I prayed, and meditated daily. I spent a lot of time focusing on my plans for the future and I achieved my goals.

I was determined to get through the pain, and learn how to be happy being alone. I was determined to change my life because it was up to me to do so. I started reading books about how to change my thought process. This step is very important, because your thoughts today will create your reality for tomorrow. I watched motivational videos on YouTube every day. I focused on who I wanted to become and I wrote down the things that I wanted to change about me. I did this because I was able to monitor my progress. It's very important for you to see things moving forward no matter how small the progress. I stayed true to myself. I believe that if you tell a lie long enough, you will convince yourself that it is true.

Now, do you see the pattern of what you need to do to rebuild yourself to a stronger person than you were before? You have to spend time focusing on you. This is the only way that you will be able to rebuild yourself from your broken place. The only way is to again put yourself first in your life. Your alone time should be dedicated to thinking about rebuilding and not thinking about what you did, or what someone else did to break you down. It happened. You can't change it, but you can change what you do from this point forward. Your thoughts control your life, and your actions build it. Spend your alone time getting control over your mind and your actions will follow.

Key Points

- It's okay to be alone as long as you're using your time wisely. Sometimes you have to be alone to find out who you truly are.
- When you're feeling alone, you must take that time to make your relationship with God stronger. Pray, read the Word, ask for guidance, and allow God to show you the next step in life. You have to spend time building/rebuilding your relationship with God.

- So many people hate being alone; it's a real fear, but it's necessary for finding yourself again. You shouldn't be afraid of being alone. That's when you have the most time to work on rebuilding yourself.
- Being in a relationship doesn't always take away the feeling of loneliness. You can have someone in your life and still feel alone. Someone's presence doesn't stop that emotional loneliness. When you are going through this stage it's because you lost yourself and it's time for you to go searching for you again.
- This is the best time for you to disconnect with the world and reconnect with God. No social media, watch less TV, and spend this time on you. Become a student of life again! Read, study, and do the research. Take the time to learn what you are supposed to do with your life!

WRITE DOWN YOUR THOUGHTS

This is self-explanatory. It is very important to write down your thoughts. Write them down on paper. Make it plain! There is something about making your thoughts visible that is quite therapeutic. Sometimes we don't know how to express ourselves verbally. Writing down your thoughts will allow you to express your emotions without being afraid. I recommend you purchase a journal and keep it with you wherever you go! Write down your thoughts everyday no matter how you feel or what you're thinking. Allow your emotions to flow from your mind onto the page. At the end of each day, go over what you wrote down that day. Assess your emotions and your thoughts. That is the best way to monitor your thought process and work on your emotions until you see that you're moving in the direction that you're trying to go.

Some people keep their thoughts to themselves. Some choose to share thoughts with others because it helps them feel better. Whatever makes you comfortable and whatever works for you, do it! You never know what may come from writing your thoughts and emotions down. One day you can write something down, and it could trigger the ultimate change that you've needed for so long. Be honest as you're writing down everything that's on your mind. No matter if it's good or bad. Honesty is the key to the development of a better you. As long as you stick to being honest and open with yourself, the growth will come faster than you know!

Your thoughts aren't meant to be kept secret. Your thoughts can cause you to go to places that you never wanted to visit. Your thoughts can intensify your pain, so you have to have some form of release. If you let your thoughts build up and you aren't dealing with them, they can cause you to lose your mind literally! Have you ever known someone that went through a traumatic experience, and they were never the same again? Part of it is due to not truly addressing the situation. They didn't truly heal! They spent all their time in a stupor of self-pity and sadness. As a result, they lost themselves in the process. Dealing with a breakup is a traumatic experience as well. Your heart and mind have broken in a way that no medicine, doctor, or drug can fix. God, time, and your actions will be the only way to become whole again.

Writing down your thoughts is to help you express and acknowledge them. Get those thoughts out of your head so they won't be jumbled up inside your mind. It helps you to see your progression day by day, week by week, and month by month. You can look back over them and see what mistakes you made, or the mistakes made against you. It can allow you to get out your anger and to not hold it in. It helps you to release the mental and emotional pain without putting it onto someone else. Thoughts are meant to be expressed in some shape, form, or fashion! You don't have to tell someone, but you do need to express them when you are going through hard times. Releasing your thoughts on paper is meant to protect you from yourself. We are our own worst enemy in life. We can talk ourselves out of happiness, greatness, and God's calling for our lives by not dealing with our thoughts of hurt and pain.

Be sure to always write down what you are thinking, good or bad! Don't be afraid to share your thoughts with someone other than yourself and a writing pad. Be sure you can trust them! Don't share your thoughts with someone that will use what you tell them today to break you down tomorrow! Go over your past thoughts to see if you've made any progress, if you've backtracked, or if you've stayed stagnant. Allow yourself to make mistakes. Don't beat yourself up over it! Learn from your thought processes of the past. Give yourself time to grow if you're open to it. Don't forget to continue to write down everything that you are feeling and thinking. Always think before you act! A moment of passion can lead you to a life of pain!

Key Points

- A lot of people can't express themselves verbally, so they write down their feelings. Writing down your thoughts gives you an outlet to express all the hurt, anger, and the frustration you are holding onto. Holding onto pain will hurt you more than the person you're angry with! Write everything down so you can release it from within you.
- Your pain may be meant to show you something in your life that you didn't know was hindering you from growing. If you don't express yourself and be truthful about how you feel verbally, or on paper, you're going to stay stagnant in your pain. You have to release it so you can see who you truly are underneath!
- Holding on to your pain can cause you to break down mentally and emotionally. When you allow all that hurt to stay bundled up within you, it's as if you're a walking time bomb! Even you don't know when that day will come when you will blow up! This is one of the ways people go crazy. They hold on to what hurt them and never release it and one day they couldn't take it anymore! So let go! Relieve some of the pressure a little each day!

- Understand this! Holding onto anger isn't going to get back the person that hurt you. Staying angry at yourself for causing the pain, isn't going to make you stronger! You have to express what you're thinking in some way! For a lot of people it's through pen and paper. This allows you to go back and see your mental state, to see if you've grown or stayed in the same place mentally!
- Writing down your thoughts is to help you let go of the pain that is consuming your life. You may not think that it will help, but I'm sure it will hurt you more if you don't try something different! I understand it's hard to express what you're feeling sometimes. That's why you write about your feelings and express it to yourself. You are the only one that can pick yourself up and move towards your path of happiness! How can you do so if you don't start creating a map to move? Your map is your words and you are creating your path with each letter that you write down.

HANDLING THE SILENCE

Silence can be therapeutic for you as you're trying to figure out your life and where to go after a breakup. It can also be devastating to your mental state, if you don't know how to deal with silence! Have you ever sat in silence and tried to focus, but you ended up thinking about the hurtful things that you never intended to think about? It's because pain welcomes silence! It forces you to think about the issue that is causing you pain. Focusing on pain only creates more pain! When you're in silence it magnifies the thoughts of what was, instead of what will be! Understand that pain comes from thinking about both happy and sad experiences. When you think about all the good experiences you've had with the ex, it brings pain! It reminds you of what was, but will never be again! Whatever you focus on in life is what increases. When you sit in silence, make sure that you're listening to your mind and not your heart. Your heart is attached to your emotions. Your emotions often lead you in the wrong direction. If your mind is lost as well, you have to put your focus back on God. If your mind and heart is gone, you've done what Chapter 1 explained. You've made someone your God!

What helped me get beyond my negative thinking was making a decision to change the way I was thinking. This is the best way to utilize silence. It allows you to focus on building your self-confidence and helps you see beyond your current emotional state. You have to be prepared to fight against what you're used to and start a new habit. Prepare your mind to deal with pressures of day-to-day obstacles. You have to use your silent time wisely, so that you can build yourself up instead of breaking yourself down! This is why you have to take back control over your mind. You may ask how to do it. I say it's in the palm of your hand! The internet! There are so many free videos and so much free information to help you change the way you think. All you have to do is take the time and search for it.

A few ways to start

- Turn off the TV and social media. If it's not helping you. it's harming you! Use your time wisely by researching ways to change your mindset. The first place I started was YouTube. I promised myself that I would change my mindset no matter what it took. That's what you have to do. You have to make a promise to yourself and keep it! Promise yourself that you will change your mindset and your life one day at a time. That's the most important way to handle the silence.
- Always try your best to listen to uplifting things. If possible, don't do anything that reminds you of the past. Remember, you're trying to get past it, not relive it!
- It's okay to cry about it (men)! Just make sure that when you release the hurt, you are trying your hardest to fill it with things that are building you up permanently and not temporarily.

Meaning, fill yourself with knowledge and the best practices of those that you admire. This is helping you build yourself bigger and better from the inside-out, and not by using sex, drugs, or alcohol! These are only temporary fixes. They aren't truly rebuilding you or fixing the problem! They are taking away and tearing you down even more.

- It took me longer than I expected to understand the concept of handling the silence. I would try to think positive, but I would always go back to my problems. I thought about my problems so much that I forgot about all the good things going on in my life! Remember, what you think about the most becomes bigger in your life. It wasn't until one day I decided that I was going to find a way to get past this pain in my life. Every time I was alone and the silence started to settle in, and I would think about all the bad things, I would go on YouTube and search for videos to change my mindset. That was when I came across Eric Thomas and Les Brown. These two men helped me get back on track! They showed me how to beat my negative silence by building up the good in me. That was the only way I was able to break free of my brokenness. That's going to be your only way as well! Use your silent time wisely by using it to build up the greatness within you!

Ten Things You Need To Focus On

1. Pray and/or meditate daily.
2. Remember silent time is growth time. Make sure you're growing while you're in a place of silence.
3. Focus on self-help and motivational materials.
4. Locate others who have successfully gone through what you have gone through, and seek counsel.
5. Remember to constantly write down your thoughts and emotions, and revisit them to review your progress.
6. Find groups that are doing things that you are interested in and join. Remember you're not alone, you're just lonely.

7. Get up, get out and do something that will help you cope with the pain.
8. Never use something or someone else to mask the pain. When they leave or it wears off, the pain is still present.
9. Don't be afraid to say *no* to your desires if they are going to set you back.
10. Don't wallow in your mess; clean yourself up, and start taking action toward your happiness.

WHAT'S ON YOUR MIND?

Willie Johnson

Rebuilding from Brokenness

Chapter 6
Letting Go

When you are able to let go, the feeling is so amazing! This is when things really start turning around for you. Letting go allows you to be free of all the pain, stress, anger, and frustrations the relationship brought into your life. For me, this was the most difficult part of the process. I couldn't let go because I didn't know how to and a part of me didn't want to! Holding on can be very dangerous. Holding on to someone that doesn't want you, or something that is not good for you will break you even more. No matter how you treat someone or what you give them, if they don't want you, it will never be enough. All breakups are different. If someone doesn't want you, letting go is your only choice. The fear of the unknown is one of the reasons we can't let go of what is hurting us. We hate the thought of starting over even when it's the best thing for us to do!

We let fear hold us back from starting a new chapter in our lives. When you hold on to someone that's asking you to let them go, you must listen to them and let go. I can't stress that enough! *Let them go!* This will benefit you and the other person as well. It will strengthen you to continue the healing process. You will start to feel your joy and happiness slowly coming back. The longer you hold on, the more pain you will cause yourself. We blame those we love for the pain we are feeling even when they have told us what we needed to hear to move on. You can't blame them for your actions! You have to be willing to put yourself first. No matter how hard it may be! The feeling of knowing that pain no longer has control over your life will allow you to see things more clearly. Understand this: You will have your highs and lows, but you have to continue on your journey of healing to become whole again! Don't be afraid of making mistakes. It's going to happen, and you have to learn from them and keep moving forward.

When you don't let go of the source of your pain, you are telling yourself, "They are all I care about and my happiness is not worth it!" You are telling yourself that they mean more to you than you mean to yourself. There are times when we hold on, not because we are still in love with that person, but we are in love with the thought of them being there. You can only take so much! There will come a time in your life when you have to stop putting more on you than you can handle. Letting go isn't about losing them! It's about finding yourself! Letting go of a painful relationship is like moving from a five-bedroom home into a two bedroom apartment! It will make you evaluate what's important to keep and what you can get rid of! It's the same with a relationship. You may keep your good memories, but get rid of anything that has no value. You have to make room in your life so that you can be blessed with bigger and better experiences. If your life is filled with clutter, you have no room for anything else. You owe it to yourself to let go, to allow your life room to grow!

Most of us don't understand that we hold ourselves back by holding on. We hold on to dead situations just because we're use to them and don't want to change. Don't complain about someone telling you it's over if you try to fix what is unrepairable. Letting go is truly hard! When you are able to let go, you'll start to see your mental and emotional state turn around in a more positive light. It's not going to happen overnight but when you reach that point of peace within you, you will say: What was I thinking, holding on to all of that mess? Letting go is the most important part of moving forward. If you don't let go, you'll continue to be locked in your past prison of life staring at your future life. You are the only person with the key to freeing yourself from your past, so that you can move towards your future. You have to be willing to ask yourself those tough questions and be truthful with your answers. Lying to yourself gets you nowhere! Being honest with yourself opens up new doors of possibilities for your life. Break down the walls of your past, and open up the doors of your future! Let go of your past, and grab hold of the keys that open the doors to your future!

What Are The Benefits?

- Be honest with yourself! Are you still holding on? The first step to solving a problem is knowing that there is one.
- Ask yourself: Are you holding on to something that's worth the pain it's causing you?
- If you let go, what will you lose? What will you gain?
- Are you willing to hurt now in order to heal later?
- Am I filled with fear or am I confusing fear with love?

WERE YOU THE HEALER OR THE WOUNDED?

What caused your unhappiness within your relationship? If you couldn't deal with it then, what makes you think you can deal with it now? I ask those questions to make you think about what you are doing , or will do if you double back to a bad situation. See, I think we have two types of people in a relationship. You have the healer and the wounded. When a healer becomes involved with another healer, you have a successful balanced relationship. They will build together and if something is broken, they want to fix it together. In the relationship, it's all about togetherness! Let's do it together, but also understand the need to do things individually. It helps keep them strong individually and stronger when they are together.

Now, when a healer and someone that's wounded get together, it's an unbalanced relationship. One is always giving more than the other. No matter the situation, the healer will put in more work the majority of the time. This is where the problem lies within this type of relationship. Eventually, the one that does all the giving will give out, and will look for their significant other to give back. Now, the majority of the time it never happens, because they haven't healed their significant other. Sometimes you may break through to them in time, for them to give back to you. With that being a rare occasion, the healer then becomes wounded and the relationship takes a turn for the worst.

Then you have two people that are wounded. From the beginning this isn't a great couple. They are both broken. They will see the bad in each other, before they will see the good! They are consumed with the negativity. This creates a problem from the beginning! They want something, but don't know what they are looking for. They want each other to make them happy. They don't understand that you have to be happy with yourself before someone can add to your happiness. So they continue to break each other down until there's nothing left to tear down. This place can be a gift and a curse at the same time. The gift is there's no place to go but up from here! If you are ready for the change, this is the best time to make it. Only you can get you out of the situation.

The healer always wants to make things right! Even if it will hurt them! They seem to be attracted to the wounded, broken down, hurting, confused, and angry individuals. It's as if they get a sense of satisfaction from trying to fix their problems. Being a savior brings them a sense of accomplishment. Although they have great intentions, most of the time they fall into the same downwards spiral with the people they are trying to heal. See, the problem with a healer is, they seem to not understand that you can't heal or fix anyone. You can only aid in their recovery. They have to want to change, be on the path to change, and then you come in and help. When you try to convince them to change because you see something great within them, it doesn't work. Until a person decides to change, the change will never occur, no matter who's telling them they need to change. Don't lose yourself while you're trying to help someone find who they are! Putting your all into someone that isn't complete can cause you so much stress, hurt, anger, and resentment. Eventually you'll become wounded, lost and looking for someone to heal you. Don't fall prey to what you are trying to help someone escape!

Key Points:

- You can't change someone, no matter what you do or say! They have to want to change and be willing to put in the effort to change.
- Don't tear yourself down trying to build them up. If they aren't ready for the change, you will eventually be in the same place spiritually, mentally, and emotionally.
- If you are a healer, understand that you will have the urge to help. You aren't meant to heal, fix, or repair. You can also hurt them by being their crutch and thinking that you are their savior. You have to let them find their own way!
- Don't be afraid to say no to someone that needs to be fixed. You can't always be there for them. Eventually you'll need someone to be there for you, because you've given out all that you needed to keep you strong.
- If you are the one that needs to be fixed, it's up to you to take the next step. No one but you can get you out of the spiritual, emotional, and mental hell you are in. If you need help, just know that the other person can't change your life! Only you can!
- You will never be able to aid in the healing process if the person doesn't know they are sick. Sometimes the best way to help someone is by walking away. Let them figure things out on their own. We sometimes think we are helping, but we actually are hindering the process by trying to be the savior. Let them go so they can learn on their own. Allow them to build their life the way they intended, not the way you wanted them to! If they come back to you, it means they were meant to be in your life. If not, you'll be happy that you didn't spend time on someone that wasn't meant for you in the first place.

TAKING RESPONSIBILITY

If you look back over all the things that you've been through, will you find that some, half, or even the majority of the pain that you felt was caused by you? I know that this may sound crazy! Many of the bad situations would have passed us by if we had just paid attention to the signs! Often, in the beginning of our relationships we see warning signs. Signs that should have caught our attention and made us think about what was to come! However, we were too caught up in a whirlwind of emotions that we're feeling. So we ignored the signs. After a while, we become afraid to walk away from the situation that we know is already over. I'm not saying that everything that happened in your relationship was your fault, but at some point you have to take responsibility for your actions. Taking responsibility makes you put on your grown man/woman pants and say, "I will do better next time." When you're at this point of healing, you are starting to see things more clearly.

What signs did you overlook? What things did you give up that you shouldn't have? Did they put their all in it like you did? Or did you put your half or none in it like them? This will help you see where you both fell short. When we're angry we can find everything that they did wrong. We forget about the things we did to hurt ourselves and them too! The sooner you take responsibility for your role in everything, the sooner you will be able to forgive, heal, and get on with your life!

Answer your why's, what's, and how's.

Why, why, God? why me?

I've treated him so well and I gave him the world, why me?

Why did she do me like this after all I've done?

What was he thinking; he had everything he needed at home?

How did she choose him over me?

How am I going to get past this?

Do any of these questions sound familiar to you? If you're not careful, you will drive yourself crazy trying to figure out why they did what they did. This is what I call, "Unknowing emotional control." This is where you allow this person to continue to control your emotions, even when they are gone. The best way to get yourself out of the "questioning" phase is to answer the questions as they come along. There will be times when you won't be able to answer some questions. That's okay! You won't be able to understand everything that went wrong. Don't beat yourself up over not knowing; you have to keep moving forward. When the time comes, you'll be able to look back and know why you went through it! I use to wonder why we made certain decision that we knew would hurt us. One day, I was put in a situation where I knew if I said yes, it would hurt me. But if I said no, it would hurt them. At that moment I realized that I was more concerned with their happiness than my own. I wondered how this could happen. How could I put someone before me, knowing that I'm not going to like the outcome? At that moment, I looked back over our relationship and I realized I'd been doing this from the beginning. I wanted so much for them to be happy! I would do things that I didn't want to do, go places I didn't want to go, and give when I didn't have, or didn't want to give.

It was up to me to put myself first and I did. I was mad at her for a long time. Blaming her for asking me to do things I didn't want to do. It was my fault because I could've said no. We all have done this. We blame others for something, when we had the choice to say no. I had to forgive her because I felt like she was the cause of my anger. All along it was me! See, I'm the healer. I always want to make sure that things are fixed and I thought I needed to be the savior for her. I gave and I gave until I was empty and couldn't give anymore. It wasn't until I said enough is enough that things changed. I took back my life by understanding that not everyone will like me. I can't say yes to everyone. It's okay to say no, if you don't want to do something, or don't feel like it. It didn't mean that I was a bad person. It just meant I was taking responsibility for my happiness!

This phase of the breakup is a good foundation to understand what's next. When you give yourself answers to questions that you've never answered before, it allows you to see things that you've never seen before. The only way you learn in life is by asking questions and searching for the answers. It's okay to ask yourself questions, but make sure you answer them honestly. This is the only way you will understand and move on. We often live our lives around our significant others. When they leave, we don't understand why we feel so empty. Well it's very simple! You cannot live your life for someone else. You live your life with someone else. When you ask yourself questions, write your answers down so you can have them as a reminder to keep yourself on track. Your life is your responsibility. No matter what others will do, or have done to you it's what you do with your actions that matters. Yes, you may be hurting from the actions of others. You have control over your emotions and your happiness! Choose your actions wisely; make sure that you are rebuilding yourself and not breaking yourself down.

Key Points

- You control your actions. If the other person tries to provoke you, how you react is up to you.
- Yes, they may have hurt you! What did you do to give them the power to hurt you? People can only break you if you let them. Yes, you'll feel some pain, but if you're broken, it's because you've allowed them to break you.
- Your decision determines how you look at life. If you feel that you are worth being first, that means you decided it. If your significant other has/had control over your life, it's because you gave it to them. You have to take responsibility and say, *I was a part of causing my unhappiness.*
- You are responsible for your happiness, period. You are the only one that can decide that you are no longer going to play the victim, but you are going to take control over your life again! The

first step to becoming happy is learning to put yourself first. If you can't master this, you will continue to feel like something is missing from your life!
- Don't be afraid to question your actions. You may mean well but when you are in a place of hurt and people see it, they will take advantage of you if you let them. Take back your power and control by not giving in to what others ask of you if it's making your situation and life harder.

SHOULD WE DOUBLE BACK

Double backing occurs when you turn back to a situation you left for an unpleasant reason. Allowing yourself to return to unhappiness in order to live in your comfort zone. Now ask yourself, *Why do we continue to double back to a place of pain for a moment of pleasure?* It always seems like when you are in a good place, the phone will ring and it's them. You know you shouldn't pick up but you do anyway. This is when you start going down memory lane and all the good old times start to come back. The little strength you had right before they called is taken away at that moment. Now you've become vulnerable to the terrible cycle of doubling back. The power of memories can cause you to fall back into a pattern of existing within pain. Doubling back is like a person with an addiction. Going back to a place of familiarity for a fix never ends well! I've seen so many people return to hell trying to find a little bit of heaven. You cannot expect something new from the same old bad situation, but we continue to try. When the relationship isn't contributing to your happiness, you have to decide whether to stay or leave. You have to decide if this is worth the stress and pain it's causing you. No one can make that decision but you and only you.

Sometimes we also are the ones that make the mistake of causing the relationship to go sour. We had a good thing but we made a bad decision. After the fact we realize how huge a mistake we made and we want to try to make things work. When we are forced out of a relationship because of our actions, if given the opportunity to go back, we have to make sure that we are prepared to put in the work to make it work. Doubling back to a good situation with the same old mindset will not only cause more pain, but it can also cause you to lose that person completely! If you truly love someone and know that you messed up, you owe it to them to come back ready to change your mindset and your actions. It's important that you only go back when you have made a definite decision that you will not repeat the past! You have to learn from it and keep it moving forward. If you aren't ready to let go of your ways, then my advice is to stay away until you are. Coming back into someone's life knowing that you aren't ready, because you aren't ready to let them go is completely selfish. That type of thinking will always lead to a bad ending! Stay away if you aren't ready! Lying to yourself and your significant other isn't healthy for either of you. The longer you lie, the longer it will take for you to complete your healing process.

I had a family member that was in an abusive relationship for years. No matter what he did to her, she would always take him back. There were times when he nearly killed her, but she was back in the house the next week or sometimes the next day. He knew exactly what to say and how to use it to get back in her good graces. After every ordeal he would treat her like a queen. He would give her anything she asked for. He would do it until she was all the way back in, and then he would go back to his old ways. One day she decided to take back control over her life. The first thing she did was leave and change her number. This stopped all communication and made it impossible for him to do what he normally did to get her back. Her actions stopped her from continuing a perpetual cycle of living in fear and unhappiness. When you are trying to let go of someone, you have to take drastic measures to protect yourself from further damage! You have to put yourself in a place where you are able to deal with your pain and mend your brokenness.

We tend to also double back thinking that the one that caused the pain can help take it away. This way of thinking is completely false. Even though their leaving you was a cause of your pain, that doesn't mean they can fix it. That's the wrong way of thinking about doubling back. They can allow you back in and treat you like a king or a Queen, but if you haven't dealt with the root of your hurt, all they will be doing is putting a band aid over an open wound. If you decide to double back, you have to understand that you can't ask them to help you tend to your wounds if you don't know where the pain is coming from. You have to deal with it first and find out where the true hurt comes from. Was it from their actions, or yours? Did their leaving you break you, because you didn't want to let go of loving them? Or was it because you were used to them? These are the questions you need to ask yourself before trying to double back and you need to answer them. If we double back for the wrong reasons, it can cause more pain than pleasure! You have to know--if you're going back--it's because you care and want to work it out. Not because you're used to being with them!

How many times have you doubled backed and were reminded of why it didn't work in the first place? Not all situations are the same. Some double backs work out for the best and some don't. I'm speaking to those of you who know you have no business going back, but you fall prey to your weakness for them. There has to come a time when you make a decision that will keep you sane. Never look back or go back to something that took from you and never gave back. Don't go back to someone who lied to you and couldn't keep their word. Don't go back if they put you through hell and promised to give you the world. These are the people that you need to stay away from. I'm not telling you to never go back to someone. If you know it's not right, then you know you aren't right for going back. Your life should mean more to you than dealing with things that you know aren't good for you. Doubling back to a bad situation will give you just that, more of that bad situation. If you're doubling back to a situation that is good for you, if given the opportunity take it, and never let it go again!

Don't let the fear of being alone cause you to go back either. Sometimes in life, you have to force yourself to be alone, so that you have enough room to see all the broken pieces! Once you are able to see them, then you'll have the time to put your life back together stronger than it was before. We have to be careful though; never put a time limit on your healing. You can't rush it! You have to be whole for you, not someone else. If you're thinking about returning to a good situation, make sure that you are truly ready. Your mindset needs to be different and your actions need to be different. You say that you truly love them, then make sure that you are giving them love and not pain. I understand that you can't stop them from feeling pain forever, but if you can control it and stop it from happening, then it's your obligation to do so. Be truthful to yourself! If you aren't ready to re-enter someone's life, don't! There comes a time in your life where you have to be truthful with yourself. If you're not ready, don't double back. If you are ready and if it's good for you, and make sure you do everything in your power to make it work.

Key points

- Don't double back if you left them for negative reasons. People don't change until they are ready to change. If they say they've changed or will change because you left, eventually they will continue the same things because it was forced without the want from them. Some people can and will change in a traumatic situation.
- If you know that you are weak when it comes to returning to a place of hurt, As I said before, disconnect yourself from them completely. No phone calls, text messages, emails, voicemail or social media. Just because you're used to it doesn't mean it's good for you.
- If you double back and they are treating you the same, you can't be mad at them. You have to be mad at yourself. You knew what they brought to the table and yet you still sat down with them.
- If they were good to you and for you but you were the one that caused pain, don't treat them as if they are wrong for not giving you another chance. You made the decision to do wrong and you

have to live with the consequences. Learn from it and never make those mistakes again.
- Don't let the fear of the unknown and familiarity keep you in a situation that's not meant for you. Fear is a belief/emotion you have towards something. Belief is what you think is true. If you change your thoughts towards something, you change the way you feel about it.

WHAT'S ON YOUR MIND?

Willie Johnson

Chapter 7
Focus On You

The best way to get back to you starts with your relationship with God. You can do everything under the sun, but until you have rekindled, or found that relationship with God, you will continue to be lost! He's the only one that can give you true insight on who you are, why you are here and what his purpose is for you. Focusing on you is one of the hardest tasks that you will have to perform. When you're so used to putting someone else before you, it is difficult to break that habit! You may not know how to do it, or where to even begin! You have to take it step by step, moment by moment, until it becomes the norm for you. Many of us are taught to be selfless, to put others first, and that's okay. However, it is also important to take care of yourself in the process! There should always be a balance between caring for others and taking care of you. A part of getting yourself back on track involves spending time getting to know the person you are right now by loving yourself, and being happy with and by yourself!

You are your greatest responsibility! Everyone else comes after. Some people may say that's not true, especially when you have kids. You are your greatest responsibility because you have to be emotionally and physically effective to be responsible for others. You have to take care of yourself before you can effectively take care of someone else. We often lose sight of that fact when we are in a relationship. We allow someone else to become our primary focus. Then we expect the same from them in return. In an ideal relationship that would definitely be the case! Most relationships are not that way. In most relationships, one person always puts in more effort than the other person. There is never a balance. Both parties never invest the same amount of time or energy into the relationship. This is why it hurts you so much when the relationship ends! Because you have invested the most!

This is the time when you have to break down the walls of what "we" like and find out what "you" like. If you don't know what makes you happy, start doing things that you've never done before! Go to places that you've never gone to before. This is similar to what "empty nesters" go through when your children are grown and move away from home. You are left all by yourself trying to figure out who you are! Start socializing more; spend time with your family and friends, but most importantly, spend as much quality time as you can with yourself. Don't be afraid to step outside your boundaries. Understand that you have only one life to live, and it's up to you to live it. Sometimes when you have done all you can, you have to allow God to give you the next step! We do not know what tomorrow may bring, but you have to be willing to live it to the fullest! Never put off what can be done today because tomorrow isn't promised. Start doing things that take you out of your comfort zone, and allow yourself to blossom into that person you never knew existed! Focus on your calling and passions! Start building your tomorrow with the actions you take today. You have the power to change your life!

So many of us are afraid of our own abilities. We talk ourselves out of our greatness and happiness. You feel that you can't do it, or that you don't know how. You also could feel like I did; like you can't do this without them. I'm here to tell you that you did it before them, so it's your choice to do it after them. My biggest mistake was I felt like I needed my ex to be happy and to accomplish what God called me to do. I was totally wrong, and if you think this way you are as well! God called "You" to fulfill the destiny He put over your life! Not you and anyone else! They can't make you happy; they only can add to your happiness. They can't live your life for you; they can only be a part of it. See, we've become so accustomed to thinking that we need someone in our life to be happy. We'll leave one situation and get into another. Looking for something that comes from within! You have to focus on you to see that God is your source for happiness. Not someone else! This is why your main focus right now should be you.

You are the only one that can build true happiness for yourself. No one can make you happy! No one can live your life for you! No one can do what God has called you to do! When you begin to focus on God, He starts to reveal things to you that you've never seen! He will open up doors that you didn't even know were there for you. Someone may come into your life, but they aren't your life. That's the problem. We try to make them our life!

We do for them first to make sure they are happy. We provide emotional and physical love to them the way that they want it, and then we think about ourselves. Your focus is off! Yes, it's okay to put them first sometimes. Chances are you aren't going to like everything they want to do, but you do it out of love. The problem is when you put them first all the time and all your focus is always on them. You lose yourself in the process of giving all of you and not being replenished. You are worth putting yourself first now! You are special no matter what you've done in your past. You can change! You have the power to change what you do from this point forward. No matter what you went through with your ex, did to your ex, or what was done to you. Your power lies within putting you first, focusing on you, and learning to love you again.

How to "focus" on you

- Build your foundation with God. You will never be complete without God being the head of your life.
- Stop spreading yourself thin to please others. Be willing to say no! This will help you keep your sanity.
- Don't spend time with people that are taking from you, but don't give anything in return.

- Accept the past! Learn from it! Used it to improve your present and future life!
- Take time to think about your decisions before you act. Be strategic!
- Understand that your happiness is your concern. No one can make you happy or create it for you. You have to take your happiness into your own hands and create it for yourself.

STOP THINKING ABOUT WHAT IF'S

What if you had all the answers to life's questions? Would you act on them? What if you were attracted to someone, everything was going great and you hit it off on all levels! Then God allowed you to see a glimpse of the heartache before it happened. Would you stay with them? What if God offered you everything you ever asked for. Then he said you have to walk away from the very person that is your everything. Could you walk away?

There will always be questions that you will never know the answers to! So stop thinking about the "what if's" and focus on "what is" and "what will be." When you're in the midst of a break up, it's hard not to say "what if," and that's understandable. I'm not saying you shouldn't question the actions of both parties, but you shouldn't dwell on it.

What if I changed the people I surround myself with? Would it improve my life, or take away from it? What if I changed the way I think, by studying and learning about the power of my thoughts? Would it improve my way of life? Learn to live in the present and plan for the future. You have no control over the past and what was! You can only change what can be! When you are able to get to this point in life, the hurt will actually turn into a great teacher! Only as long as you're willing to be an equally great student. You can use the knowledge you have gained to improve your life and the next relationship you get into. The main thing you have to do in order to prepare yourself for what's next is leaving the past in the past. The more you think about "what was", takes away from you focusing on "what is". What is happening right now in your life that's a great thing? What is God trying to teach you? This is what your focus should be on. The majority of the time we are so caught up with the past. That we aren't even interested in the present and the future!

How to leave the past in the past

- When you begin to concentrate on "what if", combat that thought with what was wrong with the relationship, and why you couldn't deal with it anymore. This will help you see why God pulled you away from them. Then think about what you want, and what you will not deal with from your next significant other. This will help you learn from the past while preparing yourself for the future. Make sure what you are preparing yourself for, is someone you can not only receive from, but also give back to. This process will not be easy at first but remember, practice makes you better, not perfect. You nor them will be perfect but will continue to get better at life.
- Don't trust your lonely feeling! You aren't lonely, you're just not used to it. This is why you start reminiscing on "what if's". If I would've just stuck in there, I wouldn't be alone! Or I really do miss them. Why couldn't it work out? This is you going through emotional withdrawals because you were addicted to their company.
- You will feel pain! Because you know that you caused this, and hate that you lost something good for you. If you didn't do anything wrong, you will think about giving them another chance even when you know you shouldn't. You may feel like you are emotionally broken and unfixable! That's not true! With time, prayer, and changed behaviors. You will start to see your "what if's" turn into; Why did I deal with that? Was I crazy? or, I'll never allow that to happen again!

Learn to use your "what if's" in a positive way. Most of us have this mental battle. We think negative about the situation first. For example; if you think "what if this doesn't work"? You will combat it with; "what if it does work"? The "Five Minute Rule" applies. Spend five minutes on the negative, and the rest of your time thinking about what to do to fix a current or future situation. We are human, and we're going to have those moments of anger and frustration. You have to fight against the negative "what if's" and focus on the positive "what if's". We can't allow the hurt to control what we do next! We have to make a definite decision. Stick to doing what's right! Make your "what if's" build your life. Not destroy it! The only way that will work, is by you focusing on things that you can change. You can change your relationship with God by making it stronger! Change the way you think and what you think! Change what you do and how you do it!

Life is too short to dwell on the past. The longer you live in the past the shorter your future becomes. I understand that it's hard to let go of the "what ifs". If you would of done things differently, would it have changed anything? You will never know! So it's best to move on from it. Things happen for a reason. No matter if it's good or bad. You have no control over what you did, but you do have control over what you can do! We all go through things in our own way. That doesn't mean you have to go through everything alone. So many "what ifs" are going to run through your mind. That's a part of the process! You don't have to focus on them. Your focus needs to be on God, yourself, and what's your next move to make your life better. Dealing with the after effects of a loss, isn't something easy to handle. With God being first in your life, time, and patience you will be just fine. I believe in you, and you should to!

IT'S OKAY TO BE SELFISH

Being selfish means; lacking consideration for others, concerned primarily with your profit, or pleasure. Some will say that it's bad to be selfish, but in this case it's totally relevant. When you have given all you can give and in return you are left empty, broken, used, or confused. It's okay to not only think about yourself! It is also okay to put yourself first! This is the time that you need to build yourself up and take care of you. I was the person that always helped and seemed to have all the answers for everyone else. When it came to me, I was lost and didn't know which way to go, or who to turn to. I surrounded myself with people that always needed me, but I didn't have anyone that could help me in my time of need. I was unbalanced and drained to the point that I couldn't pick myself up, or motivate myself when the time came. I unconsciously surrounded myself with wounded people, because I have always been "the healer."

Also, understand that you have takers that disguise themselves as givers. They will give you just enough to make you feel obligated to give to them. Nine times out of ten, what they give doesn't equate to what you give. I'm not saying that it's always the case. But if you give out more than what's coming in, you will never replenish all that's lost. Now, when it comes time for you to cater to your own needs, the takers will guilt you out of it. They will make you feel as if you're wrong for taking care of you first. You can't allow them to knock you off track. You have to stay firm on your decision and put you first! No matter if they are family or friends. If you have to let them go, don't let them stop you. When you're broken, it takes everything in you to keep going. If you have a child/children it makes it even harder to do so! This is why you can't have people in your life that are not a benefit to you, spiritually or emotionally. When you put yourself first. You have to be willing to be a villain in some people's eyes so that you can be the hero in yours!

When you feel like giving up, remember that your current situation is only for a season. You'll get past it. At first it will seem impossible to do so! As time goes on, you will become stronger and wiser! You have to make sure that you are doing it for you and not anyone else. When you try to improve yourself for someone else, it will not last and you will revert to the old you. I'm not saying it's going to be easy. But I can say with certainty, if you stay focused, strong, and don't give up on you, you will get past it!

You will come out better than you ever were before! You have the power of decision making, planning, and implementing change in your life. Understand that putting yourself first will not come easy. Most of us are wired to think of others first. At this point in your life, you have to be first no matter what! You have to be diligent, and take your time to learn how to love and care for you again. You have to be willing to fight for you, motivate you, and hold yourself accountable. Be willing to say no to others, so that you can say yes to you!

Once you are able to find the power to put yourself first. Make sure that you stay away from takers. No matter how much you love them, they always seem to take! Take and take, but never give back into you. You will be talked about and people will say that you've changed! If you are rebuilding yourself, it's good that they see a change in you. No one wants to stay the same forever! Eventually you're going to want to do things differently. Your thought process will change and the things you do will change. Change at this point in your life, is truly the most important thing you need to focus on. Make you valuable to yourself again. Understand that you are priceless and you need to treat yourself as such! If you don't treat yourself this way, How do you expect someone else to treat you that way? You desire to be first for a change. The reason others are saying you've changed is because you are no longer catering to their needs and wants. They will say you've changed for the worst in their eyes, but it's only because they aren't getting what you've always given to them. When they turn on you like that, this is an indication that they are takers. They don't care about what you need to do for yourself! They only care about what you can do for them!

Rebuilding you from the ground up means that you have to be selfish in certain areas of your life. Would you give away all the materials that you have to build your home to someone else? So that they could build their home as well? The answer is no! Your life is the same way. You can't build your life if you have given out all your tools and materials. You can't build your life spending all of your time on helping someone build theirs! You only have one life to live, and you can't spend it all on helping others find themselves if you're lost. At this point in your life, live on purpose and live your dreams! Do things that you want to do and be okay with saying no sometimes. It won't kill them if you do say no! If you don't say no and continue to give into them while trying to rebuild yourself. Then you are giving them life while taking it away from yourself!

Key Points

- Just because you say no doesn't mean that you are being selfish. You are just using your time for you. If they can't understand that, then it's good that you finally see that they don't care about you or your growth.
- If all the people around you are still asking of you when they know that you are broken and lost, let them go. They are selfish, and not in the good away. They are takers, and takers don't see anything wrong with taking. Even when it's the last of something or someone. Don't fall prey to the mindset of a taker. They will say things like; you've changed, you use to do it, why can't you do it anymore, I thought you were my friend, and you said you love me, etc. These are signs that they are the ones that don't care. Walk away if this has been a pattern of theirs.
- It's okay to let people know that you'll be missing in action for a while. Tell them you need some alone time to focus on you. Do what you need to do to spark the fire within you to change your life.

- If you have someone in your life that ask you to do things for them all the time. When you ask them to do something for you, they are always busy. They are selfish and you need to evaluate if they are worth you holding on to them. You have to be aware of takers in your life. There comes a time when you must fight for you, just as much as you fight for them.
- Just know when you start to be selfish for your own good, you will lose friends and family members. These are the ones that have always depended on you and now that the "help train" has left the station, they don't want to be around you or deal with you. That's okay! Your life will be less stressful, because you couldn't see that they brought stress into your life.
- This period of your life is for you to rebuild, love yourself, and to help you find yourself. Don't let anyone take that from you. No matter who they are! You have to start living your life for you! Stop putting your happiness and desires on hold to help someone find theirs. That's not fair to you and you're being selfish to yourself.

FORGIVING THEM AND YOURSELF

Forgiveness is the most important step you'll ever take in your healing process. Understand, you have to forgive someone for the pain they brought into your life. If you don't you are allowing them to control your life without you knowing it. Forgiveness isn't just for them. It's also for you! When you are able to forgive them for what they did to you. You take back control over your life! Most people don't understand that when you hold a grudge against someone, you are holding yourself back from advancing in your healing process. No matter how bad the breakup was, or is, you have to find the strength within to forgive them for your peace of mind. I used to hold on to grudges for so long! By the time I ran into the person again, I forgot what I was angry about! Yet, I still held onto the anger. My decision to do so, didn't allow me to move past the pain! It was as if I wanted to be angry so I could hurt her! Not knowing I was actually hurting myself. She had already moved on with her life. She was happy and having fun, and I hadn't. I wanted her to feel what I was feeling. I wanted her life to be in shambles like mine. I wanted her to lose sleep and not eat like I was, but that wasn't the case. Everything that I wanted her to feel was actually happening in my life. The worst part is, she had no idea that I felt that way! So often the people we are angry with do not know that we are still angry with them. They have moved on so they are not thinking about the past, or who they left behind.

One day I ran into her and we talked for a while. She told me she was sorry for all she did, and she forgave me for all I had done to her. It was at that moment I realized something had to change. I told her that I was sorry too, and that she was forgiven. This was another turning point for me and my life. At that moment, I let go of all the hurt, anger, and pain that I was holding on to. This is what happens when you make a decision to let go so that you can grow. Whatever you hold on to, remember you are giving that very thing an open invitation to be a part of your life. No matter if it's good or bad! The seed you sow will be the harvest you reap. I didn't understand the meaning of this statement. Until I looked back over my life to see the things that were a constant and why, I was so use to the anger! I became blind to the devastation it was causing in my life. If you look back over your life from the time that the breakup happened until this very moment of reading this book, would you say that you did more to help you or hurt you?

After all is said and done, you have to forgive yourself for what you did to cause yourself pain. What happened in the relationship that caused it to fall apart, was not all their fault. The first step to fixing a problem is to admit there is one. If that problem is you, well you have the power to change it. You have no control over how someone acts, but you do have control over how long you allow them to act that way towards you. We put ourselves through so much in the name of love, but love doesn't cause continuous pain and hurt! When you decide to walk away, or are pushed out, understand that you have to make sure to let go of what was done to you, or what you did to yourself and learn from it. If God can forgive you for all the craziness you've done towards Him and others, why can't you forgive someone else or yourself? Don't hold on to something that's killing you if you're looking for a second chance at life. Life is a teacher and you are the student. Every situation in your life is a lesson. It's up to you to study and be prepared for the next pop quiz. Learn to forgive yourself. Don't worry about what they did to you, because it's all just a test! Are you getting the correct answers so far?

One thing I can say without any hesitation. I was loyal to unforgiveness! If you did me wrong, you would have to nearly give up everything for me to forgive you. I went on like this throughout my young adulthood. Then I was put in a certain situation, I knew that this wasn't the way to live my life. If you are having a hard time with letting go, understand that you are the only person that can decide to do so. No matter how hard it may seem, you have to be willing to do it for yourself. If they cheated on you, let it go. If they lied to you, let it go. Even if they left you when you were at your lowest point in life, let it go. No one is perfect, so that means that no person's actions are perfect. We all make mistakes. No matter how much we try to do everything right, we will always fall short in one area of our lives. We have to forgive others when they do wrong towards us! Just like we would want them to forgive us when we do wrong towards them! No matter how big the problem may be, you have to decide to find a way to let it go for yourself. Not for them. Life is too short to be holding on to pain and hurt that someone has caused us. While you're sitting in your anger and misery, the one that you are mad at may be out living their life! You should be out doing the same! Live and learn to let go.

Forgiveness is a sign of strength from within. Letting go of the pain and hurt that your significant other caused you, allows you to see your life in a much bigger picture. Our lives are like a big puzzle. Every situation we go through is a part of the puzzle. We aren't able to put the puzzle together until we have gathered all the pieces. So don't look at your pain as a bad thing all the time. Look at it as part of the puzzle

God has put together for your life. Just another piece of your life is being strategically placed for the completion of your puzzle. If you are afraid to forgive because you feel like it will make you seem weak, think about what it's doing to you to hold on to the pain. Just because you hold on to something doesn't make you strong. That very thing could be the cause of your being weak! Holding on is stopping you from building the strength needed to make it to the next piece of your puzzle. Learn to love, live, forgive and grow. That's the key to a happy life. Love, live, forgive and grow. I believe in you! If I can do it, I know that you can do it! Fight through the negative thoughts. Walk away from the negative actions and stay away from negative people. What you surround yourself with, you become. So, if you are around forgiving people, you will eventually become one.

Key Points

- Forgiveness is truly meant to set you free from the bondage of your anger and hurt from your broken relationship.
- Don't be afraid to let go of the things that are breaking you. Even if you are used to them being a part of your life. Anyone that is hurting you isn't good for you.
- If you are surrounded by unforgiving people, find yourself a new crowd to hang around. You have to change the things you put in you to change what comes out of you.
- Learn to live, love, forgive, and grow. If you go through life holding on to the past, you'll never get a chance to experience the present and future. You have to let go and forgive so that you can truly live your life for yourself.
- Understand that your life is a puzzle and each situation you face gives you options for the pieces you can receive. Learn from the situation and move forward with your life or continue to be re-taught the lesson and stay stagnant in your pain. If you do the same thing constantly, it will become a habit. No matter if it's good or bad! Do you like your habits?

- Life is too short to focus on something that you have no control over. If they hurt you, forgive them and move on. That doesn't mean that you have to get back with them or become friends again. It simply means that you are not allowing what they did to hold you back from living your life. If you are the one that caused the pain, first forgive yourself and ask for forgiveness from them. If they forgive you, that's good. If they don't, that's still okay. You did your part! It's on them!

WHAT'S ON YOUR MIND?

Willie Johnson

Chapter 8
Finding the Real You

If someone walked up to you and asked, "Who are you and what are your best qualities?" Would you be able to respond without thinking about it? Often, we are quick to identify our flaws. Yet, we have to really think about what is good in us. This is because we are our greatest critics! Society has made us that way. Why is it so important for you to "find the real you" after a breakup? You often lose who you are when you are with the one you love. You spend your time doing for them, ensuring they are okay, and compromising who you are to make the relationship work. When the relationship is over, you are left wondering, "Who am I?"

You have lost touch with the person you knew before your relationship. You have become who you thought you had to be, for the sake of your relationship. You have taken on that persona, and have subconsciously created the person you have become. After the relationship ends, it is easy for you to carry on this cycle. The cycle of becoming who others say you are, or want you to be. We have to change the way we look at ourselves, for others to do the same. Your thoughts truly do create your reality. What you think about the most, you will focus on! What you focus on the most, you will believe in! What you believe in, is what you start to do! So in order to get to a place of understanding and knowing who you are, you have to first change the way you think about yourself!

It took me a while to understand that I have to search for the true me, and not believe what others think! I needed validation from others on who they thought I was. That's what got me in that predicament in the first place. I lost myself while I was in the relationship, so the relationship defined me. I didn't feel complete without her because I allowed her to become my whole life. I felt lost without her. All of my energy was spent on trying to please her while forgetting about me. This is why I say that we can't put all the blame on our ex for the hurt we are feeling. A lot of it stems from our lack of self-confidence, self-esteem, and the willingness to put ourselves first. You have to realize that constantly compromising who you are and what you believe in will slowly break you down. As a result you will lose yourself. Your opinions and actions should become your reality. Stop allowing the opinions of others to determine who you are and what you do! At the end of the day, you have to be true to who you are to be happy!

You have to take back control over your view of yourself. This happens by focusing only on your own thoughts, values, morals, beliefs, ideas, and actions. Stop telling everyone about your plans, and start making decisions on your own. Do things on your own first and let them see the progress! This allows you to discover your inner strength. This may sound funny, but sometimes we have to go through pain to bring out our greatness! Through pain things seem to become clearer. You will see that you really didn't need them as much as you thought you did. We feel we need them, when we truly don't. This is the big one! We think we love them, but we really don't! We love the thought of having them around! Learn to listen to your first instinct. Don't look past the signs and don't let go of things that you know will bother you if it continues. This is when you start compromising who you are, and it will only get worse.

When you start compromising who you are, that's when the process of losing yourself begins! I'm not saying you shouldn't compromise. When you are the one doing the compromising, you are allowing yourself to lose your individualism. You become so entangled with them that you subconsciously surrender your identity! It's okay to be a team player. Remember on every team each person has their assigned roles. In order for the team to work effectively, each player has to do their part individually and collectively. When you are the only one performing on that team, it's no longer a relationship. It's a dictatorship! Remember that you are in control of your life, happiness, and decisions. You can't consistently put someone else's happiness before your own, especially if they are not doing the same. You have to ensure that your happiness is also on track! Therefore if they decide to leave, you'll already be in a position to take care of yourself.

I've seen so many people give up on life because they felt like they couldn't go on without their significant other. People have turned to drugs, alcohol, sex, and so much more. All because of losing someone! When I was younger, I used to wonder why people would fall apart when someone walked away. I remember asking a friend of the family who was like an uncle to me. I even called him Unc! I asked him, "What made you start doing drugs?"

He said, "I made some bad decisions and one thing led to another and I wound up living on the street."

"No matter what you do in life, stay true to yourself first and then others!" He also said; "Pay attention to your actions and don't forget to love you first!" I didn't understand what he meant by that, but it stuck with me. I remembered how Unc was when I was a child. He had it all together! He was the go to person for everything.

One day I asked my mom, "What happened to Unc?" She told me, when his marriage broke up; it broke him and he never recovered. That's when it all made sense! Be truthful with yourself first and then with others.

He realized his biggest mistake was not putting himself first at times. His marriage was his life! When it all fell apart he didn't know what to do with himself. He felt empty inside and he tried to fill the void with a temporary fix. I don't want you to be like my uncle! If you feel a void in your life, sex, drugs, alcohol, and even your significant other can't fill it! No matter what you try to do, trying to fill the empty feeling inside with things will not work so stop trying. Filling the void with someone else will never work. You have to find yourself spiritually, mentally, and emotionally! You will need to first seek someone you believe in, for wisdom to make it through this. Ask for guidance so that you will know which steps to take. Ask for strength because you are weak at this time! This is the only way you will start to find who you are. Nothing, or no one, can guide you to your destination without knowing where you're going! Finding your way needs to start from within.

Key Points

- You will find yourself when you start searching on the inside first. No one will be able to tell you who you are and what you are. Finding you begins within.
- You have to pray, read, meditate, or study. Whichever one you prefer, you have to do it on a consistent basis to find you again.
- It's okay to be first in your life. When you are in a relationship, and you love or care about someone, it could seem hard to do. You have to be able to set ground rules at the beginning of your next relationship. Let them know that we have to do this as a team. Sometimes you will be the leader, and vice versa when it comes to building a happy life. It cannot be one person pulling all the weight the majority of the time. They will eventually break down and give up.
- Put God first! That's the only way to get past the pain and find you. God will mend your brokenness if you allow Him to. He will give you strength in the areas that you are weak. He'll be your direction when you are lost. The key is you have to talk to Him on a consistent basis. Allow Him into your life and follow his lead, not yours.
- Spend this time focusing on you, and not doing what you used to do. You may feel alone, but you aren't lonely. There's only

one way to fill the void. It is by finding you within God. Sex, drugs, or alcohol will make you feel incomplete. They are temporary fixes.
- Picture your heart being a broken arm. You can take medicine all day, but the pain will still be there after the medicine wears off. Until you fix the broken arm, you'll continue to feel the pain. It's the same way with your heart! You can use sex, drugs, or alcohol to take away the pain for a moment. But when it wears off, the pain will still be there. When you fix the source of the pain, you can learn to fix the problems you are having.
- Remember, you have to love yourself enough to put yourself first in your relationship sometimes. Yes, you will have to compromise and put them first as well. If you begin to put them first the majority of the time, you will need to have a serious conversation! If they don't change, then you have to make a decision. You will need to decide if it is worth the pain, or am I worth finding my happiness.

OPEN YOUR BOX/TRY NEW THINGS

Do you expect to mentally and spiritually grow? Are you mentally and spiritually boxed in with life? Often, the person you become in your relationship isn't truly who you are, or were meant to be. It is the person you thought you had to become to have a successful and happy relationship. Many of us identify ourselves by the success of our relationships. So when things go sour, we feel like failures. Now that the relationship is over, you will have to determine who you are at this moment, and who you want to become. You have to be willing to explore life as an individual. Be willing to face your discomfort and venture out into new environments. You can't pursue a better life, if you aren't willing to be exposed to something better than what you are used to. A relationship is meant to add to your already existing happiness.

Relationships should increase your spiritual and mental development. They should also bring about a new-found understanding of life.

If your relationship brings more pain, sadness, hurt, or confusion to your life, then something is terribly wrong! You will need to stop and assess your situation. You will never find true happiness in someone else. If you haven't explored a spiritual, mental, and emotional connection with God, you have hindered your individual growth. You will never truly find what you are looking for. You have to find your own happiness before you start a new relationship. This is why you need to take time for yourself before venturing into another relationship. You don't want to take any unaddressed emotional baggage and unrealistic expectations into someone else's life.

If you don't free yourself from the baggage of your past, it will stop you from exploring the future freely without hesitation. You have to let the past stay in the past. Making sure that you have let go of all the pain and hurt will open up a new life for you. When you are able to get over a devastating heartbreak, it will show you your true strength and it will give you insight concerning how to handle future events. When you are able to see an aerial view of your life, it stops you from chasing street-view dreams! You have to explore beyond your four walls of life. You have to find the strength to step outside of your box, leave your comfort zone, and find the real you. Mentally you have to free yourself from what was, and grab hold of what can and will be. This helps you see the value of your life, to identify what you are worth to yourself, and what you should be worth to others. I was afraid of being alone. I would leave one relationship and jump into the next one. I repeated this cycle for years. I went through problem after problem, until a friend told me that I would never find happiness in another person until I found happiness within myself. I thought about what she said, and realized I hadn't taken time for myself. I decided to do so. It helped me to release a lot of anger and pain I didn't know existed.

True happiness comes from within. No matter how much another person gives or does, if you're not happy with yourself, the efforts will be in vain. If you aren't using your time wisely, you'll continue to feel the pain of your decisions. It takes time to get reacquainted with yourself, and it takes time to get comfortable with trying new things. When I decided to truly let my relationship go, I didn't know where to begin. I knew I needed to find myself again. The hardest thing I had to do was to step outside my norm. I started really small! I stayed home for the first time on a Friday night. It was just me and my thoughts. It was hard! The time went by so slowly and I didn't know what to do with myself. I started doing things to occupy my time. I watched programs on TV that I had stopped watching, and it was good. After a while, it became easier. I did things that made me feel good about myself again. I started being okay with being alone and just enjoying me. I had found a new love! It was spending time with myself!

I was able to find a new love in life, by learning about myself. I spent quality time learning what made me happy. At first it wasn't easy to do because I wasn't use to being alone. The breakup forced me to get reacquainted with myself! It may sound crazy but when you lose yourself, you also lose love for yourself as well. I know that's hard to think about, but if you put someone before you all the time, how do you have time to love you? Learning to love you means that you will have to step outside your box and live life on a safe but testy, edge! Learn new ways to make yourself happy. It is necessary for the process. You have to break down the walls you've created for yourself. Allow your mind and heart to be free for happiness to come into your life again! At this point in your life, you can't put yourself in the confinements of your past. You have to be free to live life on your terms and not someone else's. You have to live with a purpose and live on purpose. Your life is depending on you to live it! So live it!

Key Points

- Don't be afraid to try new things. When you are learning about yourself all over again; it's a process and you may bump your

head along the way! Don't stop. Keep pushing until you break through every boundary of happiness!
- Understand that you are responsible for breaking away from the chains of the past. Only you can free yourself from what was in order to be free to see what can and will happen!
- You can't go forward in life looking back. You may get lost on your way to the future if you look back! Before you can go toward the future, you have to be willing to move away from the past. Meaning, you have to let go, stop holding on to what happened, and be open to explore what can happen.
- When you are able to get over a devastating heartbreak, it shows you your true strength. It gives you insight on how to handle future events. You have to find the strength to step outside of your box, leave your comfort zone, and find the real you!
- Don't ask God to give you something if you aren't prepared for it. How do you expect God to bless you if you aren't open to being exposed to it? You have to step outside your comfort zone and live a little. I'm not telling you to do something crazy, but you may have to explore different things to find your happiness in different places.
- Fall in love with you again! It's the best feeling in the world when you are happy with yourself. I don't believe we are meant to be alone forever. I do feel like we need alone time to rebuild our self-confidence and self-esteem after a breakup. You have to take your time! Don't rush the process and allow yourself to grow while you're in it.

DATE YOURSELF

How do you date yourself? I know it sounds funny, but this is very important in the process of learning what makes you happy. Dating you is the best way to learn how to love yourself again. This helps you to regain or locate valuable information about yourself—information that you lost while in the relationship or that you never knew existed. After making the mistake of jumping out of one relationship and into the next, I learned that I needed to change the process to change my outcome. When I was able to see that I was causing myself pain by not taking time for me, it was like a light switch turned on! I slowly started changing the way I conducted my everyday life. I started doing things that I wanted to do and not what others asked me to do. I opened myself to live life for me and only me! When you don't take time to "do you," you will bring all the negative bad habits into your next relationship. You must take time before getting into your next relationship. This is a critical step in healing. If you bypass it, the cycle will only continue! Dating yourself is self-explanatory. You need to treat yourself the way you would treat someone else. It may be uncomfortable for some, because they are not ready to face the issue of working on themselves. They are not ready to deal with what they've been putting off for so long, which is figuring out who they truly are.

When I was first going through this period in my life, one day it was fun under the sun and the next day I would feel lonely. My emotions were up and down. Thankfully I didn't give in to finding someone else to spend my time with. I knew if I did, that innately I would either start putting them first, or that I would be very cautious as if they were out to hurt me. I wouldn't do it on purpose, but I wasn't ready for something serious. As a defense mechanism I would be a little unpleasant. I'm sure we all have done it. We aren't trying to be mean, but we're just trying to protect our heart from another devastating situation. This feeling is like the fight-or-flight reaction that occurs when we face a perceived threat. I didn't feel like fighting or fleeing! I knew I needed time to *do me* for a while. I needed to find new and exciting things to do! That is what you need to do as well!

Dating yourself is simple. I promise that it will feel weird at first. All the things you would do with someone, you do with yourself. Go to a movie, dinner, shopping, work out, take a trip, and this is the hardest one, staying home and doing nothing. I was the type who would rather go out and do something, than to stay home alone. I really hated it! It forced me to deal with myself. For a long time I didn't feel the need to, but eventually I became accustomed to it. As I said in Chapter 4, if you do all of these things and don't deal with yourself from the inside out, it will all be in vain! Dating you is a key that will unlock the door to finding out what brings you joy. Most will leave the key to their joy locked up and won't use it for years. If you're reading this book, it means that you have located the key and you're trying to find the door that it opens. If you take your time, follow the process, and don't allow yourself to skip the steps, you'll find your door! Behind it will be everything that you've been looking for and everything that's been waiting on you! Give yourself time to grow spiritually, mentally, and emotionally.

When the time comes to explore another relationship, you know exactly who you are and what you want. Dating yourself is for your personal happiness. It is for you to learn all about you! It takes time for real change to occur. At this moment in your life, you need to make time for that change to take place. Learn to say "yes" to yourself more! You've been so used to saying no to yourself, that you don't know how to be good to you. Time waits for no one, so make every moment of life count. Do things that will impact your tomorrow in a positive way. No matter what steps you take in life, remember hurting yourself to please others will always backfire. This is your season, your season to live, grow, prosper, and be happy! Love on you, give yourself time to breathe, fight through the barriers of familiarity, and walk into the unknown. Your destiny awaits you on the other side! Go get it!

Some key factors you need to learn in this season of your growing process

- You will never find your happiness in someone else! You have to find it within you!
- Don't lose yourself while helping someone find himself or herself.

- Take time out of your busy day just for you. Make sure you are catering to yourself only.
- Be open to new adventures and new experiences. Turn over every rock in your life to see what's on the other side.
- Treat yourself as you would want someone to treat you. Prepare yourself for what you are looking to receive. This also allows you to see what you will have to offer.
- Do not bring your past into your future. You can look back at the lessons to learn from them, but you have to unpack your baggage from the past. It is essential to do this before you walk into the future with someone else.

TRUST YOUR INSTINCTS

When you first got into your relationship, did you look past all the signs? Signs that told you to walk away, or to stay? So many times we are given the signs that this is not the right situation, or this is not the right person for us to be with, and we push it aside, because we are satisfying our wants. I'm sure we all have done this. I know I have! I have looked past the brightest signs that I should walk away. I wanted what I wanted at the time, and wasn't paying attention to my needs! How far will you go to please your wants and forget about your needs? Your needs will stay consistent throughout your life, but your wants will always change. We always want new and better things, but we don't need them. This is why you should always trust your instincts! When you have that gut feeling that you need to walk away, but you are afraid of how it will make them feel, that is you putting them before yourself. You're not allowing your instincts to be a guide for you to make the right decisions.

I'm not saying that our instincts are always correct. If you see the signs, have a weird feeling about it, and you still proceed to go along with it, it's on you! We can't let our fear of being alone push us into a situation that we aren't ready for and shouldn't be in. Your instincts were given to you for a reason. It's like having a third eye to see beyond the obvious. Sometimes our instincts are so accurate with what we need to do, and not do! It's virtually impossible for you to say that you're confused about what you need to do. Not listening to your instincts can get you into situations that you wish you were never in! You end up in a situation where you want to walk away, and yet, emotionally you're caught up and you feel obligated. If it's hurting you more than it's helping you and you aren't married, the decision to walk away will be much easier than if you are married. Relationships are based on this belief system of: "I trust you and you trust me." If there's no trust in the relationship and something is wrong, but you can't put your finger on it, it's your instincts kicking in telling you to pay close attention to what's happening. It's letting you know that you need to protect yourself. Have a conversation with your partner to get on the same page. From that conversation you'll know what needs to be done.

The relationship did not work out. Now you are spending time learning about you. You are allowing yourself to be reacquainted with who you once were and who you want to be. This helps you heighten the awareness of your natural instincts. You will become more in tune with yourself! You are able to connect with yourself on a much deeper level. You have taken away everything that was holding you back and blinding you from seeing yourself. A relationship is meant to enhance your life, not take away from it. If things aren't feeling right from the beginning, you have to trust yourself. Believe that what you are feeling is for your own good! Instincts are a guide to help you make good decisions. It can keep you from going into the wrong situation and help you recognize good situations. There was a time in my life when I was so focused on building my future that I could tell the type of people to not to be around, what situations or places to not be in, and things I should and shouldn't do. I was so in tune with my connection with God that my instincts were impeccable. Once I got off track and stopped spending my early morning hours praying, reading, and meditating, that's when things started to fall apart for me.

As I look back over my life. I see where I went wrong and what I did wrong. I've started doing the things that I once did before. These practices help me make the right decisions. I understand that things get hard sometimes. I also understand that life may be pulling you in different directions. That is when you should buckle down. Focus on your relationship with God and yourself! When all hell has broken loose in your life, you need to become whole. Start waking up a little earlier if you can to get focused. Wake up, give thanks, and be grateful that you are able to see another day to get it right! Pray or meditate on your goals and the bigger picture. Set intentions for your day! Read things that motivate you to do better in your life and career. Study the successful people in the field you want to be successful in. This is putting your life in order and making you the priority. It's getting you focused and breaking down all the walls that were blocking your natural instincts from guiding you. Whatever you focus on the most becomes the biggest influence in your life! Focus on and follow your instincts! They will guide you in the right direction! Your life is designed for you to prosper in every area.

Key Points

- Only you can get yourself back on track to your true happiness.
- Your last relationship may have broken you. If you direct all of your pain, hurt, frustrations, and anger on reconnecting with you, everything else will fall into place! You will heal better and be stronger than before.
- You have to know what direction to go in if you're wanting to leave the place that you're in. The way to do that is to focus and sharpen your instincts by focusing on the source. God!
- I believe that every situation in life teaches you something. If you continue to fight the same battles, I feel that you haven't learned your lesson yet. Every lesson gives us more insight on what to do and what not to do.

- Learning your lesson helps you see things in a different light! It means that you're building up your natural instincts, which will show you how to look at things differently. Learning lessons helps you not repeat the past!
- If you aren't connected with God, you have lost your source of instincts. Everything you do from this point will be due to your own fruition. It's on you!

WHAT'S ON YOUR MIND?

Chapter 9

Time to Heal

Now that you've dealt with all of your hurt, pain, frustrations, and anger, you have let go of the past. Now it's time to heal! Through every storm in life, there's a lesson to be learned. If you've truly moved forward and your life has spiritually, mentally, and emotionally changed, you should be joyful. Everyone doesn't make it out of their storm at the same pace! Some let the storm destroy them and take over what little life they have left. One thing you can truly be happy about is learning that you are stronger than you knew you could be. You've learned what needs to be done if this comes up again in your life. Let's pray that it doesn't! I hope your next relationship is everything that you ever wanted and needed. Let's pray you find that special someone, or they find you. This time in your life is all about you! At this point, your main focus is to continue to grow in every area. When you stop thinking that you are lost because the relationship didn't work out, you've transformed your weakness into strength!

Often, we beat ourselves down more than the world and we compound our problems! We can be our worst enemy by criticizing every detail while forgetting about everything that is right! When you've learned that no matter what you go through, you can grow through it, at that time you learn to use your pain to grow. Now you've become your greatest supporter. You see that your life wasn't just your relationship, and that there's more to you! The reason you couldn't see it before is that you were too busy focusing on a relationship that was destroying you emotionally! You couldn't see all that you could offer to yourself and to others. Your greatness, your pain, and the things you've been through in life aren't just for you. They're meant to help others as well. Always use your pain to help you gain more strength to deal with your current situations and future failures. It is easy to fail! How you get back up is the hardest part! You might have failed, but look at how strong you are now! You got back up after life knocked you down. Now, you're stronger than you were before!

When a damaging relationship ends, most of us feel like we've lost everything. In retrospect we truly gained from losing. You've gained the purpose for life that you lost while trying to find the purpose of your broken relationship. You gained freedom to be yourself again and put yourself first. You've gained clarity regarding the path that you are meant to take. Don't always look at loss as a bad thing. Think of it this way. You asked God to bless you with a job, more pay, and better benefits. You did all the research, went on the interviews, and waited for someone to call you back. You hoped that they'd call you back to offer you the position. In order for you to accept the position, you have to let go of the old job! To move on, you have to let go of all the frustrations, the people hating you, no promotion, or not being paid what you were worth! Don't forget about the things you've learned. You will need those lessons to help you prosper in your next position! That's the way life goes. If you are in a place that isn't building you anymore, do what needs to be done to move on! Don't forget what you've learned; use it to make your current venture in life better than your past!

Your healing process will start when you are ready to let go but not forget. If you're still angry at them for where you are, you aren't ready. When you can say to yourself: "It hurts, but I know I'm going to be okay?" and you mean it in your heart, that's when the healing process begins! All of the hurt and pain you've been through wasn't to break you. It was to build you up! It took me so long to get past my pain, because I didn't give myself time to heal. I masked it by bringing someone else into my life. I thought that they would be able to fill the void that I was feeling. When we broke up, I felt lost and alone because I had lost myself. I didn't know who I was anymore! A mentor told me one day, "until you start living for you again, you will always feel lost!" I realized that in order for me to feel whole again, I needed to find me again. That's when my healing process began. I went searching for me and not someone else!

Your healing will begin when you start looking in the right places for the right things. No one can tell you how to heal. People can only provide guidance or advice. It's all up to you when, and how you heal. You have to start within first. You can do everything to fix what's on the outside. You can dress it up, make it smell good, and look flawless. You can do all of those things and still be a mess internally! Healing first starts with you dealing with what broke in the first place.

Figuring out the real problem is the hardest part! When I messed up my relationship, I thought her leaving me was the part that hurt me the most. So, I focused on that! Later on, I realized that what I did to make her walk away was what hurt me the most. I caused this hurt to myself, and blamed it on her as if she caused it! A big part of healing is taking responsibility for the things you did that got you to this point. I know we may think we are perfect at times, but no one is perfect! When you can see your wrong, it makes it easier to address it. We must evaluate ourselves before we can evaluate someone else. We talk about all the bad they did, but seem to forget about what we did! This isn't easy, and yet it is necessary for the process of healing to work the way that you want it to! You control your happiness and God controls your joy! Happiness comes and goes, but joy is an everlasting feeling!

Key Points

- Healing will not start until you are truly ready. No one can tell you how or when. It's all up to you!
- You have to take responsibility for what you did to get you to the place where you are.

- Take responsibility for your role in the failure of the relationship.
- Focus on you and you alone; don't bring anyone into your mess. Deal with you first before you try to deal with someone else.
- Stop thinking that you are a failure because your relationship didn't work! Sometimes we have to lose things that aren't good for us, to make room for things that are good for us.
- You have to let go in order to grow! Never forget: You have to let go of the hurt, anger, and pain of the past in order to be happy in the future.
- Always work from the inside out. Don't make the mistake of trying to fix what you look like, and neglect what you feel like!
- Don't search for happiness. Search for joy! Happiness is a feeling that comes and goes with the waves of life. Joy is a way of life. It comes from the heart, not the mind!

YOU'RE OKAY

Can you truly say that you have let go and are now in a place of growth? I asked myself this question on a regular basis, when I was on my path of healing. It's okay to assess your progress. In fact, I encourage you to do this! Although my progress was slow, I kept it moving forward! Sometimes I would take two steps forward and life would knock me three steps back! I didn't let it stop me and I kept going! The further I traveled on my path, the more I became okay with the process. I wasn't moving as fast as I liked, but at least I was moving in the direction of growth. I had to learn that it's okay if you aren't moving as fast as others. You have to be okay with the process. Yes, some people will seem to heal faster than you! That's okay! Keep in mind that they might have not endured the hell that you did! They could be skipping steps as well. Everything is not as it seems! When you skip parts of the process, no matter what you do, you will have to come back to complete them! You can't cheat or finagle yourself out of the healing process! Have you ever run up a staircase and tried to skip a few steps? Did you fall? When you picked yourself up, did you take your time the rest of the way? You didn't want to repeat that feeling of falling again. After that experience, you looked at stairs differently! Didn't you? You realized that the stairs were meant to help you! Yet, if you try to skip them, they also can hurt you! That's how the process of healing works. When you try to skip a step, it may seem good at that moment, but life has a way of bringing that step back around!

We think that we have to be strong all the time. That's the farthest from the truth! When we are open about how we feel and stop trying to be so strong, it allows us to move one step closer to our goal of having true joy! I once read that when you cry, your body releases endorphins that can improve your mood. Did you know that? Crying relieves your body of pinned up stress. That's why when you cry, sometimes you feel better right afterwards. When my relationship didn't work out, it devastated me! For a long time I wouldn't allow myself to cry. I would say that it was their loss, and I'm stronger than this! I would feel the onset of the pain coming . I would get that choked up feeling in my throat. I knew that tears were coming and that they were coming with a vengeance. I would do everything in my power to stop them!

People started to say that I'd changed, or that I was changing. I wasn't my happy go-lucky self anymore! I walked around like it was me against the world! I felt like no one could understand the pain that I was feeling. I wouldn't talk about it and I kept it bottled up inside! I saw my ex one day, and when I got back to my car, I couldn't hold the tears back any longer! I began to cry like a little baby. I cried so hard that my head started hurting! After I stopped crying, I felt like the world was lifted off my shoulders! This was the first time after my breakup that I felt like I was going to be okay. I realized in that moment, that it was truly okay to be vulnerable! It helps you get the ball rolling when you're trying to heal from within. You have to let out what's hurting you!

I never thought I would say this; but my pain turned out to be my pleasure. The things I learned about myself were priceless! I don't think I would've learned without going through what I went through. Have you learned things about yourself? Were they what you never knew until you experienced your heartache? I'm not saying every hurtful situation you go through will turn out to be a pleasurable experience. What I will say is that in every test there's a lesson to be learned! Think about every situation that you go through in life. You may not like it, but I'm sure you can learn from it! That was one of the ways I was able to keep pushing through. Even when I didn't feel like it! I thought about what I was able to learn from it, and how it would help strengthen me as an individual. That's how we all should look at life. No matter the situation, we can learn from it if you understand the test. You will learn the lesson! When you learn the lesson, it will help build knowledge and wisdom! They say that knowledge is power. I say what you do with the knowledge gives you the power! When you take this process of thinking, and apply it to your life, it will make every situation okay!

Key points

- It's okay to let go of the control that you think you have over your emotions. Allow yourself to be emptied of the pain and hurt from your breakup. Allow yourself to be filled with the joy of knowing that you will be okay!
- Don't be afraid to talk about your pain. You aren't the only one going through it!
- It's okay to not know the reason for your breakup. Just focus on what you did, and what you can do next!
- This is for the men. When we don't release our tears, it hurts us and prolongs the process! God gave us tear ducts for a reason. It's okay to use them!
- Take what you've learned from your pain and turn it into the fuel that you need. Let it push you to becoming a better you!

The best way to show someone what they've lost is by making yourself better. Better than you were when you were with them!

YOUR STRENGTH

If you've taken your time, and spent it on rebuilding yourself, you have seen how strong you truly are. It's not easy to come back from a broken place, mend your fractured heart, and change the way you look at life! Through all of the pain and lonely nights, Crying until you had a headache and almost giving up on love—you have found your strength and kept going! When you are able to say, "I've made it!" despite the mountain you had to climb, is the best feeling ever! Then you look back over all that you put yourself through, and you laugh and say, "I'm stronger because of it!"

We often short change ourselves because of someone else's view of us! Never allow yourself to be weakened by the thoughts, or actions of others! No matter what your ex may think about you, you are stronger than you know! Ever heard the saying, "You never know what you have until it's gone"? That's how you need to look at the situation. Never devalue yourself to give value to someone else! Never take on all of the blame for the breakup if you didn't cause it! If you did cause it, on it, learn from it and grow from it. You should know that you are stronger now than you've ever been! You can't make everyone happy. If someone dislikes the way that you're working on you, then so be it! Even if you're the one that cause the breakup, don't let that make you feel like you aren't good enough to be loved. Everyone makes mistakes. Just make sure to learn from yours; never do it again, and keep moving!

Life isn't easy. Yet, you've made it this far! You've been able to fight through all your battles and come out on the other side. Some will say that I haven't won all of my battles. You may not win all your battles, but you will win the war! It's about perseverance. The hardest thing to do when you're heartbroken is to look at the situation from a different perspective. Changing your mindset is the second most powerful thing that you can do in your healing process! You have the power to alter your outlook on negative circumstances. You should know the first most powerful thing by now: having a personal relationship with God. If you make these two actions a part of your life, you will come out better than you were when you went in! Your willingness to put in the hard work, will reward you in ways that you've never seen before! Getting that person back won't make you stronger. Getting revenge won't do it either! Focusing on your relationship with God first and changing your mindset will give you the kind of strength you never knew was possible! You will be able to handle the disappointments of heartache differently. You will know that you can make it through!

The more you focus on all of the bad in life, the harder it will be for you to build yourself up. No one can give you strength. Only God has that kind of power! What you focus on, is what you become. When you focus on that power, that's what you get in return! If you're blocking God from showing you what's next, you're blocking the correct steps in your life. Yes, you will stumble and make mistakes. If you can stay focused on moving forward, it will build character and understanding! Ultimately, you're building a better and stronger you. When you take your focus off what happened, and put it on yourself, you will begin to see the areas in your life that need work. Focus on you and work on the things that others can't see!

By doing so, you will strengthen yourself from within. I'm not saying that you should neglect others, but you must be a priority in your life! Not being a priority is part of the reason you're in this predicament. No matter what happened yesterday, tomorrow gives you the opportunity to do better! True strength comes from within. Your inner strength has nothing to do with how big your muscles are. It has everything to do with your mentally and spiritually state! Either way, when become stronger within, people start to notice something different about you and you'll feel it. Remember what I said in Chapter 7. You have to be willing to focus on building yourself up! If you're no good to yourself, how will you be good for anyone else? To answer that question: *You can't!* If you're a mess, nine times out of ten you'll give someone the same energy. Don't worry about what happened with the relationship. Start thinking about what you want for yourself, so that you'll be better prepared for your next relationship.

Key points

- You have to be okay with change. No matter what you do in life, in order to grow, you have to be willing to change.
- Understand that your strength comes from within. You have to make God a priority. Put your all in Him, and he will strengthen you beyond your understanding.
- Learn to change your mindset towards life. There are many books and websites that focus on changing your mindset.
- You now can trust yourself! It's okay that you failed in your relationship. Remember your mistakes, learn from them, and take away the good to apply it to your next relationship.
- Make sure to take time for yourself to keep you strong in the areas where you are weak. You have to be on top of it at all times. Old habits die hard, but they can be permanently destroyed by the creation of new and improved habits.
- Never devalue yourself to give value to someone else. This is so important! When you tear yourself down to build someone else up, where does that leave you when they depart? It leaves you feeling alone, lost, broken, angry and confused.
- Remember, what you focus on is what you become. If you don't like the way you are, then change your focus.

START LAUGHING MORE

They say laughter is good for the soul. Therefore it's important that we laugh. I love to laugh all the time! You have to have fun in life, even when life seems unfair. You can't let your hurt keep you down. It may seem like life is out to get you, but try your best to find something to smile about! You will have your good and bad days. That's a part of life! Try to overpower your bad with the good. Laughter is such a healthy thing. It can help reduce stress and lower blood pressure. It can also help you boost your immune system to aid in fighting illnesses. I can stop right here and end the chapter with that. Laughter makes you feel good! Most of all, it costs you nothing to laugh! What more could you ask for? Something that naturally helps improve your health, release the anger, and the hurt. Laughter does all of those things and builds you up all at the same time! This is why it's important for you to have people around you that add to your life and not take away from it. When you are in your healing process, you truly don't have much or anything at all emotionally to give out. Having others that will give into you is a plus! True friends are the people that make you laugh, have fun, and keep you from wallowing in your mess. Laugher also strengthens you from a mental aspect. It helps you look at life in a more positive way. When you spiritually have joy, you become emotionally happy, which in turn helps motivate you to become physically happy as well.

Laughter is a great way to help you let go and push you to continue your process. It makes you feel like everything will be okay no matter how it looks! Personally, it helps me when I make others laugh. Most people look at karma only for the bad in life, but it goes both ways. I try my hardest to always give out positive energy, so that's what I get back. Even the good word says, do to others as you would have them do to you (Luke 6:31). There's something about treating others with kindness and care that helps things seem to be okay. If you have negative people around you, distance yourself from them. When you're taking steps forward, you don't need someone talking about what used to be! You need people that will speak life into you. Life is too short to think about everything that happened and to not focus on what you want and can be. You have to get out and live life. Try new things and be willing to make a fool of yourself. You only live once, but you can experience so many things while you're on this journey of enlightenment. You have to be willing to do things you've never done before so that you can experience a joy you've never felt before!

I've learned that it's up to us to change our outlook of a bad situation. When you mess up in life, sometimes you have to laugh at yourself! It's okay. You will make mistakes, but you can't let what you did hold you back from what you can do. Yes, you may have caused yourself to experience pain from your decisions, but you can't allow your pain to stop you from having joy! If you learned from it, laugh about it and move on. That's a great way to look at it! Learn, laugh, and move on! Stop dwelling on the past pain and mistakes. Learn to live life for all the great things it has to offer. Stop allowing what you did to take away your happiness. It was just a lesson to be learned! Don't spend another minute of your life dealing with the "what if's," and start thinking about what can be. Learn to laugh at mistakes, smile at the naysayers, and live your life to make yourself happy for a change!

Key Points

- Learn, laugh, and move on. Learn from your situations, laugh about it, and move on from it.
- Don't worry about what people may think about you or say about you. They don't control your life. You do!
- There's always a lesson to be learned from a bad situation. Learn it, own it, and change it!
- Keep your distance from negative people. They will suck the happiness right out of your life!
- Treat others how you would like to be treated. Karma goes both ways. What you do will come back to you, no matter if it's good or bad.

- Be willing to make a fool of yourself even if it's going to take you out of your box. You have to learn to live and stop existing!
- Life is too short to spend it wondering about what you did, or what was done to you. The past is the past! You can only live in the present and prepare for your future.
- You only have one shot at life. Are you willing to misfire until you hit your target. Meaning: Are you willing to make mistakes until you get it right? Or, are you just going to give up?
- Laughter is good for the soul! Don't be afraid to do more of it at your expense. Sometimes you have to laugh at yourself when life doesn't go according to your plan. This too shall pass!
- Laughter isn't just to have fun! It helps heal you from within and helps build your immune system to fight illnesses. Laughter can also give you a better outlook on life!

WHAT'S ON YOUR MIND?

Willie Johnson

Rebuilding from Brokenness

Chapter 10
Acceptance

Acceptance is the best stage in the process. It may not feel like it, but this is an important step to help you start your process of healing. When you are able to accept your situation, you are able to focus on internal change. Acceptance is the ending of one chapter and the beginning of a new one. It's your letting go of everything that happened to you, but learning from it at the same time. All those nights of your crying, and asking yourself, "Why" will start fading away. You were stagnant before because you wouldn't let go. The end of something always initiates the beginning of another. When we are able to accept that what was may never be again, that is when we can take complete control over our lives! Most of us prolong our process of healing, because we didn't want to accept that things were over. Not only are you holding yourself back. You are also creating more hurt than pleasure! Why hold on to dead weight? Why waste your energy on a shattered relationship that's unfixable? When I couldn't let go of my ex, I thought that I was still in love with her. After someone apart and taking time for me, I was able to let go. I realized then that I wasn't in love. I was comfortable. When I was able to accept that, I felt like the world was lifted off of my shoulders. I was able to grow and blossom into the man that I am today.

The greatest adversary of acceptance is being comfortable with dysfunction. Most of the time we know we should leave. We are so afraid of the unknown that we will allow ourselves to continue to stay in our hurt. We are so afraid of change! We justify our not leaving by saying things like: "It takes too long to get to know someone," or "What if I meet someone and they are worse than what I have now?" These are excuses to stay in your pain because you're used to it! I used to wonder why people would stay in a mentally and physically abusive relationship. I would hear people say; "I love them!" Every last person that I came in contact with over the years, said the same thing! A few of them got out of their abusive relationships, and they were able to break free of the control that person had over them. I asked them: *Why did you stay?* They either said that they loved them, or that they were afraid of them! They confused fear with love. Once they were able to break free, they realized that it was better to be alone than to stay. You might have been beaten down emotionally and physically by your ex, but you weren't yourself! You fought against your mind with your heart. You let your emotions lie to you! You kicked rationale and logic completely out! You made excuses for why you shouldn't leave, knowing that it was the best thing to do. Once you are able to mentally break free from the emotional prison that you've put yourself in, you will be able to accept that the unknown is better than what you currently know!

Being able to accept your present situation shows growth and wisdom. We take hardship for granted, but it prepares us for what is to come. For every level there's a bigger devil. Often when you are at a place of peace and clarity, there will be new challenges. Does it ever seem like more things come at you? This is because you aren't letting life hold you back from moving forward. Acceptance is a decision! You are choosing to accept what was, and not let it hinder you from what will be. Your two greatest tools of growth are decision making and action! In order for them to fix what's broken, you have to use them together. They go hand and hand. You can decide all day to do something. Until you act on that decision, you will continue to be stagnant! Yes, the relationship ended! You made mistakes, and they made mistakes! Now that you have gotten past all of your heartache, you have come out better than when you went in!

One of my closest friends is going through a breakup as I'm writing this book. When I was going through my confused and hurt stage, he would let me sleep on his couch. Not because I didn't have my own place to stay, but because I had to get away from my place. The silence was deafening! See, at the time I didn't know how to control the silence. All I did was think about us, what I did, and why. He would tell me, "You have to let her go bro, and focus on yourself!" He never told me how to do it. He and a few other friends would try their best to keep me busy. It wasn't enough! All that they were doing was helping me mask the pain. It wasn't helping me deal with it head on! Eventually, I was able to get past it and rebuild myself. Now that he's going through it, I told him the same thing he told me! I told him to let her go and to focus on yourself. The difference is, I was able give him advice on how to do it and what not to do! We all have different ways of dealing with things. There are certain things that don't work for any of us. Those things are: jumping straight into another relationship, drinking, and doing drugs. Also, acting like we aren't hurt, not dealing with the pain, and using sex to make you feel better! These things only make you feel better for the moment. Neither of these actions will help you move forward with rebuilding you. Again, it actually hurts you more in some cases. Masking the pain will never solve your problems. It will only prolong the process of healing. You have to be able to find your strength, face your hurt, and fears head on. Accept that it's time for you to move on!

Back to my friend! I told him to not answer the phone if she calls or texts. As a matter of fact, I told him to block her number! I also told him to stay away from places that they frequently went to. I told him to stay away from the things that would make him think about her. I advised him to take this time to rebuild himself! I also told him not to sit in silence without being productive, because it would make things worse at first. Try your best to have fun. Hang out with friends that will encourage you, and don't talk about your relationship. Pray every day for guidance to become whole again. If you have pictures, videos, clothes, or anything at your place that she left, send them to her, put them in storage or throw them away! If she wanted them, she would've taken them. You don't need any constant reminders of what was. You need things to help you see what can and will be. This will help you get past all the hurt and pain that you are feeling. These things will help you get to the point of being able to accept that it's over and start moving forward.

Your life depends on you and your actions. You can't rebuild if you don't accept that the past is the past. The past cannot be changed. You need to focus on what's in front of you right now! That's what you have control over. Acceptance plus focus and action equals a new you! Keep your head up, chase your dreams, and keep God first in everything that you do. If you do those three things, you'll see that you had the power all along. We give our power away every time we do something to make someone else happy! When you are able to accept that you need to be first when it comes to happiness, that's when you break the hold that your pain has over you!

Key points

- When you are able to mentally break free from the emotional prison that you've put yourself in, you will be able to accept that the unknown is much greater than what you currently know.
- Acceptance is a decision to choose what happened and not let it hinder you from what will be!
- When you are able to accept what happened, you are able to change what your actions will be if there's a next time. Hopefully, there won't be a next time!
- The greatest adversary of acceptance is being comfortable. If you are comfortable with misery, she will always keep you company. You have to be willing to break free from what you know is hurting and killing you and explore things that will heal and save you!
- Being able to accept things and learn the lessons within your troubles means that you have gained wisdom. Be willing to open

your mind and heart! Focus on what's ahead of you, not on what's behind you! If you go through life looking at the past, you will crash right into your future and destroy it.
- Your two greatest tools of growth are decision making and action. You can decide all day to do something, but until you act on it, you will continue to be stagnant! If you don't decide to do something, you'll never act on it. You have to make a definite decision and act according to your choices!
- Masking the pain will never solve your problems; it will only prolong the process of healing. There are certain things that don't work for all of us. Jumping straight into another relationship, drinking, drugs, and having sex will only make you feel better for the moment! You have to be able to find your strength. Face your hurt head on and accept that it's time for you to move on!
- Your life depends on you and your actions! You can't rebuild if you don't accept that the past is the past. The past cannot be changed!
- Acceptance plus focus and action equals a new you! Stay focused! Give yourself time to learn how to move within the space you're currently in and start acting on your dreams.

WHAT DID YOU LEARN?

When it's all said and done. You have to sit back and look over the path that got you to this point. It's hard to say what will learn at the beginning of your heartache. When you get past all the hurt and pain, you are able to see the great things that came out of your pain. Yes, it broke your heart, but you didn't let it break your spirit! Yes, you felt like giving up, but you found your inner strength! You kept pushing forward until you broke through your pain and used it for your growth! When I reflected on my path, I remembered saying that I would listen to the advice from others more. I'm not saying that I will do exactly as they say, but I will take it into consideration. I will use the advice and figure out how it would play a pivotal role in my life. I had a few friends and family members that tried to help me prepare myself for what was coming. Unfortunately, I didn't listen! They went through everything that I was going through. They saw that I was making the same mistakes that they made. They tried to help me avoid them, so that I wouldn't feel what they felt! They realized that it is possible to avoid pain if you don't do certain things. We are so hard headed when it comes to our life. We think we know it all! I've learned that life is a good teacher, and yet that doesn't mean that you have to be the one learning the hard and hurting lesson! Someone else can teach you what they've learned in heart aches if you're open to listen!

Would you go through life being a teacher in order to teach others how to avoid pain? If it means that you have to endure it as well? Or, would you rather be a student and learn from the failures and successes of others? Some of us spend most of our lives being teachers, and some spend most of their time being students. We have to understand how to balance the two! Some things you can't avoid learning, but you can prepare yourself for it. What you're feeling right now, or what you have felt isn't new to the world. I'm sure there are family and friends around you that have been through what you are going through. They have learned how to deal with everything that you've felt and will feel along the way. At this moment in your life, you have to be the student and learn from them! Don't be afraid to open up and ask for help. Trade out your role as teacher to be the student until you've broken down the walls of anger, hurt, and bitterness. Yes, some things you have to learn on your own. If you're willing to be vulnerable, life is willing to guide you to a stronger you.

I learned that it was up to me to deal with my misery. No matter what someone told me, I was stuck in my misery. I felt like life was unfair! I was so angry! I couldn't see that my anger was causing me to hurt more and longer. I had to let go of acting like I was in control. I broke down and asked God to help me lose my pride and show me the way. I learned that God was waiting for me to let go, so that he could take the steering wheel of my life! I don't know where you are emotionally right now. If you appear to be in control in public, while you are a mess behind closed doors, it's time for you to let go so that you can start growing! All you're doing is prolonging the process. Don't be afraid to learn from someone else's mistakes. I did and it helped me find a part of me that I didn't know existed! I also learned that we are our own worst enemy. We will fight to stay in a relationship that's killing us, but we will blame someone else for the murder weapon. If they say that they need a break, we get mad but we want to stay in the relationship! When they say that they need space, nine times out of ten they mean it. It's best to let go, walk away, and work on yourself!

When your significant other tells you anything of that nature and you fight to hold on, you're fighting a losing battle. If someone doesn't want a relationship and they stop fighting for it. That's the only time they cannot fight and still win the war! If you're the only one fighting, I would suggest you stop and focus on you! This is another reason why we are so lost when the relationship doesn't work out. We've spent so much time fighting for them that we forgot to fight for ourselves! We forget about how important our happiness is to us, even if we did wrong! If you are the one that caused the pain, I am not saying don't fight for it. I am saying if they have expressed that they don't want you, or need some time, that's when you stop fighting! Your focus should automatically shift to focusing on you. It's easier said than done. You have to push yourself toward your happiness! If you don't, you'll find yourself broken and trying to rebuild on a cracked foundation. If you haven't learned by now what you should be doing, I'll remind you. Stop focusing on a dead situation, if you know you can't breathe life into it. If they need time, give it to them. Take that time for yourself as well. It's better to build when you have all the tools for construction, than when they are taken away. Meaning, if you listen to them when they say that they need time, or don't want to be in a relationship and you give it to them. That saves you from giving your all and not getting anything in return. You won't feel used, lost, broken, and empty. This feeling occurs when you have given your all and it wasn't returned.

At this point you should understand yourself more. All the pain and struggle you went through should've helped you realize how strong you are and can be. Never allow a situation like this to break you to the point that you are unfixable! Life is too short to spend all of it dwelling in your misery. When you give someone the power to control whether you're happy or not, you give them complete control over your happiness! Never give your power away! You can love and trust again one day. Just remember that you should never hurt yourself to make others happy. If you are able to receive something that's equal to what you are giving, then you have finally reached a point of living.

Key Points

- When your significant other tells you they need space, give it to them! Trying to fight for them when they aren't fighting for you, will hurt you in ways you never imagined.
- If they're showing you that they aren't interested anymore and they completely change the way that they treat you, it's best to walk away! If this has been going on for a long time and no change has come, let it go. You are hurting yourself and making the situation worse.
- I know it's harder to walk away in a marriage, but we know when it's truly over. Sleeping in different beds, not speaking to each other, and feeling like a stranger in your own home. You have to make a decision. Is it helping us or am I giving breath to a dead situation?
- Stop focusing on a dead situation if you know you can't breathe life into it. If they need time, give it to them. Take that time for yourself as well.
- Don't be afraid to open up and ask for help. We feel like we are strong enough to deal with emotional pain like we deal with physical pain. The difference between the two is as long as you keep a physical wound clean and bandaged, it will heal. With

emotional wounds you can't bandage or patch it up; you have to rebuild and reconstruct.
- Stop spending so much time fighting for them if they aren't fighting with you. Let them go so the sun can shine on you and help you grow. Your happiness is more important than your happiness with them!
- Never allow a situation like this to break you to the point that you are unfixable. You're beautifully made and you are priceless! Even if they tell you you're worthless, know that God took his time to make you! The best way to prove your worth is to focus on bettering yourself inside and out. Let them see the diamond that you are! You needed to be cleaned and polished!

WHAT TO DO NEXT TIME.

Let's say that there's a next time. You have to remember everything you've learned from your past. You can't let your heart hold you back from moving forward. You'll be well ahead of the game, if you understand that you can't put your significant other's happiness before yours all the time. If you are placed in this position again, do you think you would be mentally prepared? You can't control whom you love, but you can control what you do when you're in love! When I ask if you will be prepared, I'm not talking about emotionally. I'm speaking about mentally! You can't control your heart, but you can control your mind. You have to mentally stay strong throughout your relationship for your own sanity. You control what goes in and what comes out. It's up to you on how you want things to go mentally.

The only way that you can truly prepare yourself for a next time is through your thoughts. When it comes to love, 99% of the time our heart is stronger than our mind. You're so in love even during hard times and you fight through it all, because you are doing it together. It's a different story when it comes to the pain of a breakup. This is when your mind takes over and goes into overdrive. You can't stop thinking about the good or the bad. It seems like your mind plays tricks on you. The moment you think about something good, you think about the breakup and it intensifies the pain. Emotionally, you can start to feel better and feel like you've taken five steps forward until something happens to make you start thinking about them and it knocks you back ten steps!

You control your actions in life by controlling the way you look at life. Therefore, to control both you have to change what influences you allow in your life. If you caused the pain by cheating, think about what you did before you got to that point. When you started the process of getting to the act of cheating, I'm sure you thought that you shouldn't do it, and yet, you allowed your emotional and physical desires to overpower what's right. As a result of that, you were caught and left alone. What was the first thing that you started doing? It was first your thoughts and then your actions that got you into your mess that left you alone. Your mind is more powerful than you may know. This is why you have to do everything in your power to control your mental processes, what you see and hear. It controls your actions and ultimately it controls your life.

I learned this the hard way as well. I became a better man when I grew to understand more. I didn't learn how to handle my pain. I was stuck in Chapter 3 "Don't Date" phase for a long time. My understanding of dealing with pain before dealing with someone else wasn't a part of my thinking. I would leave one relationship and jump into the next one. I didn't know that I was hindering my growth with my actions. All I thought about was what and who to do next. I was a good dude, but I had a terrible way of dealing with my pain. This is what kept me in Chapter 3 for so long. I wanted something that my mind and heart wasn't ready for! One day someone I look up to said that I was causing my own pain. I thought I had everything under control. I was so wrong! I realized that something had to change in me if I wanted things to change around me. So I started searching for ways to change from within! Most people feel like they can control their hurt. They think that they will be okay once they find someone else. They don't realize that they are only suppressing the pain which will harm them more than they know.

If you don't deal with the breakup when it happens, you will deal with it later on in a different form. That pain can manifest in so many different ways. It can come back as a physical illness. It can hinder you from being loved again or loving again. It can also devastate your mind so much that you can lose it! This is why you have to protect your mind and heart. This will let you see what is hindering you from moving forward in life and love. The Bible says in Colossians 3:2, "Set your minds on things above, not on earthly things." You have to stop focusing on what is, and put your focus on what will be. Yes, the pain that you feel from your broken relationship isn't the end of your world! It's only the end of a chapter in your book of life. You can't let one chapter define the way you will live the rest of your life. Your mind has ways of playing tricks. If you aren't able to decipher what's true, you could find yourself mentally lost. That is why God asks you to put your mind on him. He's your guidance to a better you!

I use to wonder if our minds told our hearts to love, or if our hearts told our minds to love. It seemed like when I fell in love, I thought about everything she did for me. I also thought about how it made me feel when she did it. I didn't know if my thoughts provoked love, or if my heart felt love before I thought about it. Your mind is the gateway to love and pain. You must control what goes in and what comes out. So, next time make sure you are preparing yourself mentally to deal with what comes emotionally. Understand that we can't control what the world brings. We can only control how we react to it! Keep your mind focused, for the next time that you are ready to love. Don't be afraid to put yourself first sometimes! Take time for you and build a stronger relationship with God. Make sure that he's the head of your life, thoughts, and actions! Read and study ways to change your mindset. You can also study books on the human mind. Force yourself to step outside of your box and do things that you aren't used to doing to build yourself up.

Key Points

- The Bible says in Colossians 3:2, "Set your minds on things above, not on earthly things. You have to stop focusing on *what is* and focus on *what will be*.
- You can't let your heart hold you back from moving forward. The more you focus on your pain, the more you will intensify your hurt.
- You can't control whom you love, but you can control how you love. Putting someone else other than God before your wants and needs all of the time, can bring about devastating results.
- You control your actions in life by controlling the way you look at life. To control both, you have to change what influences you allow in your life. If you only allow a mess to come in, a mess will be the only thing coming out. You imitate what you see and hear. If you don't like your reactions, change the source of your actions.
- If you caused the pain by cheating, you have to understand that your mind was the starting factor. Your emotions were the deciding factor! If you learn to control your mind, you control your actions.
- Your power lies in your actions for the future. You first have to let go of the past so that you can grab hold of your future. You have the power to change your tomorrow by what you start doing today. How's your tomorrow looking today?

LET GO. NEVER FORGET!

Many of us are afraid to let go of everything that we know. You should let go, but I'm not saying that you should forget. You should make room in your life for your future love and not keep it cluttered with your past love. Letting go of your past isn't to free them from your grasp. It's to free you from the grasp of your past which is stopping you from moving into your future. Your future isn't centered around anyone. It's centered around you and your growth! That is what your focus needs to be on from this point forward. We all have gotten caught up in love and felt like we couldn't go anywhere else. Remember that you have a purpose and you can't waste your life living in the past! Letting go is releasing all the hurt and pain that your past caused you. It is allowing yourself to be free to love you and others again. How do you expect to love someone else if you don't know how to love yourself first? This is the time for you to learn how to love yourself unconditionally again. It's actually easier said than done when you've neglected yourself for so long. I've learned through my trials and errors in life that everything that hurts will help you be better in the future. If you are able to put the puzzle pieces together, that is even better!

Never forget what you endured because it shows you how strong you are. You shouldn't hold on to what hurt you. When you hold on to what helped you get past the pain, and let go of the hurt, that is when you've learned the art of letting go but not forgetting. When we come out on the other side of our brokenness, we tend to say that it made us stronger! I like to think of it like this: We were already strong; we just needed a situation to show us how strong we truly are. I think that letting go was the hardest step for me. I didn't like to fail at anything and letting go made me feel like I failed at love. I don't know about you but failure for me really sucks! I needed to understand that mistakes weren't failures. They were my steps to build a more successful relationship and life next time around. I never forgot about the things that I did, or how it made her feel and how it made me feel. I let go of all the pain it caused me. I was familiar with the pain and I knew how to handle it. It wasn't good for me and it was dead weight weighing me down! Have you let go of what has been holding you back from moving forward? It's okay to let go because it gives you room to move and grow.

Your happiness depends on you letting go of your past. How can you be happy with life, if all that you know is misery? Why do people complain about the pain, but won't let it go? If it's hurting you, release it so you can move on! You're the only person that can change the way your mind and heart heals. You have to keep yourself busy while you are rebuilding. It will help you with combating the negative feelings of not being good enough. That's a big pill to swallow when you are feeling inadequate and unloved. The longer you hold on to those feelings, the longer you will feel the pain from them. Holding on to the past is like putting your hand in burning hot water. It's going to hurt you no matter how you do it. Some things and people in life aren't meant to be permanent. They are meant to teach you a lesson and then you move on from them. We tend to make a temporary situation into a permanent one. Then, we wonder why it causes us so much pain, stress, hurt, and anger. It's because you've learned your lesson. Now it's time for you to part ways and move on. It's not about you being mean. It is about the cycle of life! You learn how to apply what you've been taught, and then you can graduate to the next level. It's just like school. Your teacher isn't your permanent teacher. He or she is in your life for a season to teach you a lesson! Next, you will be tested on what they taught you. If you fail the test, then they will continue to teach you until you've learned that particular lesson. Life is the same way! You are taught a lesson; you learn it; and then you are tested. If you ace it, you can move to the next lesson. Each lesson in life prepares you for the next level in life.

Remember, letting go doesn't mean you're giving up. It means that you are choosing to grow from your stagnant state of thinking. Your life is waiting on you to live it! It's up to you to pursue it. Never allow your past to stop you from living your future in love and life. You are wonderfully made and you are meant for someone! Your ex may not have been the one to experience your love for a lifetime. Maybe you taught them how to get it right the next time, or vice versa. Everything in life happens for a reason. You will just have to learn your lessons and use it to build you into the man/woman that God called you to be. No matter how things may look in the beginning, you must allow life to teach you. Learn the lessons and apply it to your life. Hopefully, your next relationship will turn out much differently! Let go of your pain, anger, and the hurt. Grab a hold of your joy and strength, because you are meant to be happy! No matter what the world may bring your way. Remember to put God first and yourself second. Follow his path and his purpose for your life. Everything else will fall into place! If no one has told you that they love you, I love you!

Key Points

- Letting go of your past isn't to free the other person from your grasp. It's to free you from the grasp of your past that is stopping you from moving into your future. If you want things to change, you must first change the way you do things.
- I've learned through my trials and errors in life. Everything that hurts will help you become better in the future. If you are able to put the puzzle pieces together, that is even better! It's not easy, but you are the only one that can solve the puzzle that's called your life, and God is guiding you through this maze. You can't do it on your own! Every time you try to do it on your own, you'll end up hurt or broken. Don't try to control the uncontrollable. That's all up to God!
- When you hold on to what helped you get past the pain and let go of the hurt, you've learned the art of letting go, but not forgetting. It's easier said than done, but you have to do it. You'll continue to walk and run in a circle if you do not let go. You'll never be able to love you or someone else while holding on to pain. Anything associated with the pain will automatically push you away from that person or situation.

- Your mistakes aren't failures. They are lessons to teach you how to be successful. Never believe that lie even if you're telling it to yourself. You will make mistakes in life and relationships, but that doesn't mean that you're a failure. You're just learning your life lessons.
- Your happiness depends on you letting go of your past. How can you be happy with life if all that you know if misery? You have to ask yourself, if holding on to my misery is more important than grabbing hold of my happiness. You have to decide which one is more important.
- Some things and people in life aren't meant to be permanent. They are meant to teach you a lesson and then you move on. If it's hurting you, or holding you back, why are you still stressing about letting it go? You are stressing over letting go of the source of the hurt not knowing that you are compounding it by stressing over it.
- Remember, letting go doesn't mean that you're giving up! It means you are choosing to grow from your stagnant state of thinking. Your life is waiting for you to come live it. It's up to you to pursue it!

WHAT'S ON YOUR MIND?

Rebuilding from Brokenness

About the Author

Willie Johnson is a Certified Life Coach that has a unique way of connecting with you. From a very early age, he had a love and passion to help others see the greatness within them. Most thought he would be a preacher but he took another route and became a Motivational Speaker. Rebuilding from Brokenness was written not only from others experience but it also comes from a very personal place in his life as well. As he was writing the book, he was experiencing every chapter. He went through the emotional ups and downs but he knew his pain had a purpose. When he felt like giving up, he thought about you, how it would affect you if he didn't finish what he started. Although it was hard, he was able to push through and come out a better man for it.

His purpose of writing Rebuilding from Brokenness was to help others understand that the process after you are broken is very important. You can't allow yourself to stay stagnant mentally, spiritually, emotionally or physically. If you miss a step, you may miss very important information needed to continue the process. He knew one of the major problems most have is, they'll grab onto something or someone else to mask the pain and that's the worst decision you can make. You have to deal with it head on or it will always be a part of your life. He explained the only way to get past it is to deal with it, get over it and move on. Willie Johnson's passion to care about people runs deep and he will continue his work with rebuilding you from the inside out.

Contact Willie Johnson at www.iamwilliejohnson.com